# Thriving in a Male-Dominated Workplace

# Women *at* Work

*Inspiring conversations, advancing together*

The **HBR WOMEN AT WORK SERIES** spotlights the real challenges and opportunities women experience throughout their careers. With interviews from the popular podcast of the same name and related articles, stories, and research, these books provide inspiration and advice for taking on topics at work like inequity, advancement, and building community. Featuring detailed discussion guides, this series will help you spark important conversations about where we're at and how to move forward.

**Books in the series include:**

*Making Real Connections*

*Next-Level Negotiating*

*Speak Up, Speak Out*

*Taking Charge of Your Career*

*Thriving in a Male-Dominated Workplace*

*You, the Leader*

**Women *at* Work**

*Inspiring conversations, advancing together*

# Thriving in a Male-Dominated Workplace

Harvard Business Review Press
Boston, Massachusetts

Printed in the United States of America

10 9 8 7 6 5 4 3 2



Library of Congress Cataloging-in-Publication Data

Names: Harvard Business Review Press, issuing body.
Title: Thriving in a male-dominated workplace.
Other titles: HBR women at work series.
Description: Boston, Massachusetts : Harvard Business Review Press, [2023] | Series: HBR women at work series | Includes index.
Identifiers: LCCN 2022022619 (print) | LCCN 2022022620 (ebook) | ISBN 9781647824617 (paperback) | ISBN 9781647824624 (epub)
Subjects: LCSH: Sex discrimination in employment. | Male domination (Social structure) | Success in business. | Women employees. | Employees. | Cooperation.
Classification: LCC HD6060 .T47 2023 (print) | LCC HD6060 (ebook) | DDC 331.4/133--dc23/eng/20220815
LC record available at https://lccn.loc.gov/2022022619
LC ebook record available at https://lccn.loc.gov/2022022620

ISBN: 978-1-64782-461-7
eISBN: 978-1-64782-462-4

The paper used in this publication meets the requirements of the American National Standard for Permanence of Paper for Publications and Documents in Libraries and Archives Z39.48-1992.

# CONTENTS

SECTION SIX

## Build a Better Culture—Together

## INTRODUCTION

# Fighting the Disparities

by Amanda Kersey, producer of *Women at Work*

Toward the end of 2019, *Women at Work* cohost Amy Gallo and I visited Olin College of Engineering in Massachusetts. Olin's student body is slightly over half female—an extraordinary gender ratio for an engineering program. We were there to hear from two seniors, Ana and Elena, who would soon enter a workforce that was far less equal and far more inhospitable. We wanted to ask them what sort of support they had gotten in school that they hoped to receive in their jobs and how they envisioned their futures. Having read up on the career outlook for women in STEM fields, I wondered whether Ana and Elena understood the extent of the challenges awaiting them, whether they had started to develop the skills to deal and a plan to succeed.

Elena told us she'd come to view the women on Olin's faculty as role models. "It's amazing to see them come in and teach class every day and know that I could go do that," she said. Finding the same level of gender representation, she added, would also be a "big thing when I'm looking at places to work." Given that 8.7% of mechanical engineers in the United States are women and that the aerospace industry, which she hoped to join, has been stuck at around 20% globally for the last 30 years, finding a company that met her expectations likely would be difficult.[1]

Interning taught her that she'd need to vet companies not only for how many women they employed but also hidden stressors within the culture. During one internship, a female employee had complained to her about how the men regularly got coffee together without ever inviting the women. From that point on, Elena noticed as well. "This isn't something that everyone sees immediately," she said. "When I think about places that I'm going to work long term, how do I notice these dynamics before I say yes?"

Ana, meanwhile, was preparing to join the 1.7% of mechanical engineers in the United States who are Asian women. "I think about being in a predominantly white space and how that also makes it difficult in some cases to speak up," she said. The reticence that can result from feeling a "heightened sense of difference" is one of the harmful effects of environments being segregated by sex and race.[2]

Unfortunately, Elena's experience isn't unique, and Ana's concerns aren't unfounded. Women in male-dominated fields and workplaces, who already face exclusion and isolation, must deal with stereotypes that compound the stress. For instance, men in these spaces often assume that women (especially nonwhite women) aren't sufficiently competent, even if they're highly educated and skilled.[3] Women put in extra effort to strive for perfection, fit into uncomfortable norms, and prove themselves as valuable team members—yet they struggle to gain the respect they deserve, get credit for their work, and attain leadership opportunities.

An email our podcast team received from a mid-career engineer speaks to the frustration we've heard from many women:

> *To get to where I am in my career today, I have spent a huge amount of time and energy pushing for more responsibility, agonizing over how to act in situations, exceeding expectations on tasks, and fighting for recognition. At the same time, I feel like the men around me just have to do "normal" things and produce "normal" work to get the big projects, the boss's trust, and the big promotions.*

Women regularly fight against these unfair practices so that they can accomplish the technical, essential projects that they aspire to and that their companies hired them to do. But for all the ways that male-dominated workplaces undermine them, many still want to be there—and intend to stay. And despite the frustration, they have resolve. In

2021 I listened to a webinar for women in construction that discussed the progress they've made in an industry where their representation is approximately 13% in Canada and 10% in the United States and the European Union. One of the panelists summed up their resourcefulness: "Ladies, this is construction. Sometimes we won't have a seat at the table, but bring your folding chair!"

This book is for both women sitting in a folding chair and those at the table.

For those in a folding chair, the book offers facts and validation about the challenges women face; an argument for seeing yourself as an asset, not an imposter; and advice for building a strong reputation, identifying allies, and responding to bias. It also has answers to questions that our listeners—whether they work in sales, software, or national security—have asked over and over: How can I improve my experiences at work? Be seen and valued? Progress in my career?

While specific cultures (both geographic and corporate) have a significant influence on each woman's experiences, this book highlights some of the universal challenges women in male-dominated workplaces face—and provides solutions. Through research, conversations with experts, and detailed personal accounts, it explains why these systems persist and how industries and organizations need to change. Most of all, it has tips and advice to help you thrive until that happens.

But you can't do it alone—nor should you try. As one of our listeners, who for 17 years has been the only woman in a small department of a large utility company, wrote to us, "It's very isolating because there's no one in this section of the company that I can commiserate with or band together with, so I am all on my lonesome to call things out and try to change them." This book will equip you to connect with the few women around you, as well as with the men and leaders who can play a part in your growth and development.

You'll also learn to navigate some particularly uncomfortable experiences, including overt bias and sexism. While many companies are tamping down on such attitudes and behaviors, they're still a widespread problem. One of our listeners, a woman in the mining industry, recounted a meeting where she was standing next to a female colleague who was preparing to speak. As she reviewed her talking points on a notepad, which included a to-do list, a male colleague reached over and added "bake a cake" to the list. And another woman, a sales executive in construction, told us, "Going out for drinks . . . I hear the men talking about other women in the bar. . . . I don't know how to respond to the constant sarcasm; after all, it always has more than a little truth to it." You'll learn when and how to speak up in these situations—even if that inappropriate comment is coming from your boss.

While all of the advice is intended to help you as an individual, researcher Teresa Cardador emphasizes at the start of the book that "the onus really needs to be on organizations to change their cultures, change the reward systems that they have, or change how they value and reward men over women in these kinds of environments." For that reason, in the last section of the book we call on everyone sitting at the table to build a better culture with those around them. Men and women alike must come together to break up overly masculine cultures, pay attention to the discrimination and harassment happening to women (especially those who are not white), and enact real change.

Since our podcast launched, many women have written in to say that our conversations have not only validated their experiences but have also given them courage and hope. Many times the positive impact that women say our podcast has had on their lives has left me crying at my computer. One woman in a deeply sex-segregated field and workplace told us that for years she'd been sexually harassed and had been scared to speak up. "Your podcast gave me a lot of courage, and finally I told the sexual-harassment committee about the issues," she wrote. "Things are starting to change. You told us that we need to change our cultures. I think my action is a small but solid step to change our culture in our fields."

We hope this book will help you do the same.

SECTION ONE

# The Challenges We Face

# 1

# Subtle Stressors That Hold Us Back

A conversation with Teresa Cardador

It can be difficult when you work in a field or workplace where men significantly outnumber women. Gender bias can run rampant. You can feel like an outsider on your team. You may feel like you have no control over your career path or growth. It takes resilience just to survive, let alone thrive.

Teresa Cardador, a professor at the University of Illinois Urbana-Champaign, has documented the stress female engineers commonly feel from working with mostly men, as well as how they cope. In this conversation, Amy Bernstein, Amy Gallo, and Nicole Torres, cohosts of HBR's *Women at Work* podcast, talk to Teresa about the subtle stressors facing women in male-dominated workplaces and how to overcome them.

**AMY GALLO:** We've heard from students of engineering about the stressors affecting women preparing for a career in the field. What stands out to you as the major challenges that women need to overcome when you hear accounts like these?

**TERESA CARDADOR:** The first one that stands out to me is the feeling of minority or outsider status in a profession that seems to be reserved for men. Men think of themselves as part of the club, and women who are just starting out feel like outsiders who have to work their way in. Some women I've talked to have mentioned how it's hard to speak up. You feel like you're not being listened to. You might feel excluded. There are definitely feelings of having to prove yourself or even questioning yourself—*Do I really belong here?*—because you feel like you're outside of the club. Dealing with these kinds of subtle stressors takes a lot of effort, and it can often be draining.

**AMY BERNSTEIN:** What about the confidence gap?

**TERESA:** The confidence gap is really complicated and gets back to the perceived outsider status in this profession. Women often assume that men know more than they do. The cultures are often more masculine and competitive, and men may speak more confidently. We've heard from students in the field that women tend to discover over time that they *do* know as much as the guys do, but it lowers their confidence in the short run.

**NICOLE TORRES:** Of the women that you've studied, how do you find that they deal with these stressors?

**TERESA:** Well, in addition to these stressors, we have uncovered what we consider to be another one. Let me describe that a little bit first, and then I'll talk about how women address these issues.

In some of my research, we've found that the roles that women perform in engineering can often seem less valued within the profession as compared to the roles that men play. Everyone is familiar with the idea that engineering is a sex-segregated occupation, right? There are more men than women. But in the research that my colleagues and I have been doing, we've noticed some patterns of sex segregation within the occupation itself.

In engineering, there are two kinds of recognized skill sets. One is what you think about generally, which is the "hard" technical skills. The other is the "soft" professional or managerial skills—managing, multitasking, communicating, and so on. The former is often more valued in engineering and more associated with what it means to be a "real" engineer, whereas the latter tends to be viewed by engineers as more peripheral and less associated with being a real engineer.

Research has shown that women are less likely to pursue roles in the purely technical side and more likely to be found in roles with strong professional skill requirements. Now, to be clear, these professional skill roles are still very highly technical, but because of the way that the purely technical roles tend to be more valued in engineering, the roles that women play—these perceived "peripheral" roles—tend to leave them feeling less valued and often less respected, which creates stress.

What my research *doesn't* show is that as a result of women moving into these managerial roles, they're more likely to have access to top-level management roles in engineering organizations. Those are still dominated by men, unfortunately. So women aren't getting the fast track to high-level managerial positions; they tend to get product management, project management, and managerial engineering positions.

There can be a real bump in pay associated with moving into a managerial role. But what my research shows, including a study with Patrick Hill of Washington University, is that women who move into these managerial roles report lower perceptions that their work is meaningful, lower identification with their engineering colleagues, and greater work-life balance challenges. This could be because the managerial roles allow for less flexibility about where and how they spend their time, or maybe they require more face time. These women also report greater intention to leave the profession, and they generally get judged more harshly on their technical ability.

So we think that, in an environment where women are already stereotyped as less technically competent, being disproportionately present in managerial roles reinforces gender stereotypes about their technical ability and their competence in the eyes of their male colleagues.

**AMY B.:** And you're not seeing that negative piece of it with men who advance into managerial roles?

**TERESA:** We haven't really studied in depth the experience of men in managerial roles specifically, but I can tell you what some of the study's interview data was telling us. The short answer is that men do not seem to be penalized as much in terms of perceptions of their technical ability and technical competence. For men, there appears to be this kind of both/and perception that they have the technical ability as well as these broader professional skills. But for women, there seems to be a perception that one comes at the cost of the other.

**AMY G.:** So the perception is that women move into those roles because they don't have the technical chops. Whereas if men do it, it's because they have these great additional managerial skills they can add to the mix.

**TERESA:** Exactly.

**AMY G.:** You also study how women deal with a lot of these stressors, whether it's being pushed into managerial jobs, feeling less confident, the overt bias, or the microaggressions. What do you see women who are succeeding in these fields doing differently?

**TERESA:** The first thing that is important for women to understand is the nature of the gender stereotypes and biases that they're confronting. A lot of women who enter the profession have a sense that these kinds of stereotypes and bias are things that maybe their moms experienced but aren't something that affects them. So many women are surprised and dismayed to see—especially as they progress in the profession—that these things still go on and that they will experience overt forms of discrimination and more subtle forms of bias.

In terms of moving into managerial roles, one of the things that I often suggest to women is to evaluate your preferences as you consider what roles you want to take within engineering. Some of the women that I've talked to actually say, "Yes, I am very interested in pursuing a managerial role because it fits with my preferences. It fits with the way that I like to do work. It fits with my interests." Other women tell me that they started out on a more technical track, but over time they were mentored by very well-meaning mentors and managers into managerial roles because they were identified as having skills that might be relatively rare in those contexts—very good communication skills, very good skills in terms of organizing other people—skills that maybe their male colleagues were not seen as being as strong in. These women say they are mentored into these more managerial roles, and then they get on a path where those managerial experiences become path dependent. They actually report that the organization is grooming them to take on those kinds of roles.

When I talk to women about managerial versus technical paths, I often encourage them to think about whether the paths that they're being mentored into are actually a good fit with their preferences, or whether they're choosing these roles because someone in their organization is encouraging them in this direction, even if it isn't something that naturally fits their interests.

If you're on the managerial path for a long time, it can be difficult to get back on the technical path because the skills in those areas are so specialized. So if you're in a managerial role for a while, it might be easy or not surprising to lose a little bit of technical specialization. That's not to say that you can't get that back, of course, but because of the role requirements, a lot of the women engineers I've talked to report to me that you don't have to have as much technical specialization to pursue the managerial roles.

**AMY G.:** Given what you've just described, it seems like the advice would be to set it up as an experiment, so that the transition back won't be so painful or difficult if they decide that's what they want to do.

**TERESA:** Yeah. There are women in my samples who remained on the technical track, and what some of them said is that even if they had managerial aspirations later, they were very strategic in wanting to stay on the technical career path for a minimum number of years, in order to develop and retain the technical chops needed to have that flexibility later on. They didn't necessarily talk about it as a strategy to protect themselves from being stuck in a particular role; they just felt like they needed to have a certain level of technical sophistication before they thought about moving into a managerial role.

**AMY G.:** One of the tactics we've heard recommended in these environments is to play nice in order to get things done. How has that worked for women that you've looked at?

**TERESA:** This is a classic thing that I hear all the time. The upside is the potential for connection—women enjoy interacting with people in the workplace in a relational way. But the downside of having to do this work is that it's a form of emotional labor. It takes a lot of effort and can be time-consuming. I'm doing research with some colleagues where we use the phrase "performative niceness" to refer to how women are required to engage in a certain set of behaviors that literally add hours to their week.

It also can undermine your authority if you're seen as too nice—particularly in male-dominated occupations, because the gender stereotypes are so exaggerated there. Women have to thread the needle or walk this fine line of playing nice in order to avoid the penalty and get what they want, but it can sometimes undermine their authority. A mixture of being perceived as nice and authoritative is really needed, and that isn't always easy to achieve.

**AMY G.:** You related this to threading the needle. What are your tactics for doing that?

**TERESA:** It's hard. Some of the research that I'm doing and some of the work that's out there shows that it gets better with advancing tenure. With advanced tenure, many women feel that they have proved their competence and they have to engage in less of these proving behaviors. So it does get better.

The other factor is that it's less of a challenge for women when they have established relationships, which, again, is correlated with tenure. But as a result of those two factors, you maybe have to engage in these proving behaviors a little bit less. In established relationships, you might get more of a pass for not being nice all the time. If people know you and they've worked with you day in and day out—say, if they work with you all the time in the operating room versus being one of many teams that rotate through with a team of surgeons—then it's easier. If you have a bad day and you're super direct with someone, or raise your voice, or show those kinds of assertive behaviors that might be penalized in other contexts, people might be more willing to give you a pass because they think, *OK, we know Teresa. She's a real person, and she's just having a bad day.* Once you form relationships with people, that tends to help.

**NICOLE:** If a woman is in an organization where she's starting to feel like she doesn't fit in, and she's thinking about leaving or trying to make it work, what do you suggest that she do? Should she just quit, or can she try to make it better for herself?

**TERESA:** I get asked for career advice a lot, and I'm always hesitant to give it because there are so many factors that go into making a decision about what's right for you. Obviously, if the situation is not sustainable and someone is miserable and unhappy, then I would encourage her to look for environments where she feels that she's equally valued and maximally supported, environments that are friendly to both women and men. If she really felt like the environment she was in wasn't sustainable, I might ask a series of questions to help her understand whether making a move was right for her.

But a lot of the solutions that we think of in terms of how women should navigate the situation really put the onus on women to change their behavior, change their environment, figure out how to talk to people differently, or change their attitude in some way. These can be helpful in terms of coping, but none of those recommendations feels satisfying to me, because women's lack of awareness, behavior, or attitudes are not the real problem.

For these issues to really, truly change and for women to benefit, the onus really needs to be on organizations to change their cultures, change the reward systems that they have, or change how they value and reward men over women in these kinds of environments. Focusing on those broader cultural and systemic issues—that's where we're going to make the most change.

*Adapted from "When You Work in a Male-Dominated Industry,"* Women at Work *podcast season 4, episode 9, December 9, 2019.*

# 2

# To Succeed, Women Need More Visibility

by Shelley J. Correll and Lori Nishiura Mackenzie

Companies in male-dominated industries are failing to retain their female employees. A study by Jennifer Glass of the University of Texas at Austin and her coauthors found that women leave STEM fields at dramatically higher rates than women in other occupations.[1] After 12 years, 50% of women in technical industries, predominantly engineering and computer science, had switched to other fields; 20% of other women professionals had done the same.

The highest-profile losses in tech are those at the senior level. These women often are less satisfied with their careers, perceive that they are unlikely to advance at their current organizations, or believe they must change jobs in order to reach the next level.[2] As one technology executive explained to us, "We have some very capable women in the middle management and junior VP levels, but they leave our firm to advance their careers as they continually get passed over for promotion."

What can companies do to stop the departure of senior women? One critical but overlooked strategy: Make sure that women have the right kind of visibility within the organization.

We led a thought exercise for 240 senior leaders of a Silicon Valley technology company, asking them to identify the most critical factors for success at their level. The group agreed on track record and skills-based factors: a history of delivering results, a technical depth of expertise, and the ability to manage a technical team.

Next, we asked them to name the most critical factors for *promotion to* their level. A new top criterion emerged, eclipsing all others: visibility. More than technical competence, business results, or team leadership ability, these leaders agreed, visibility is the most important factor for advancement.

We then conducted performance calibration reviews in three companies and six focus groups with midlevel and senior leaders to understand how they rated individuals and perceived opportunities for advancement in their companies. According to our observations, visibility is a complex interaction of perceived skills (particularly technical and leadership ones), access to stretch assignments, and being known—and liked—by influential senior leaders within informal networks. All three are necessary for advancement.

Across each of these categories, however, we observed gendered dynamics that systematically disadvantaged women in achieving visibility, potentially limiting their opportunities for promotion and keeping them from the senior levels of their organizations.

## Visibility of Valued Skills

The visibility of one's technical skills influenced how valuable specific employees were perceived to be. This presented a conundrum for women. Since they were less likely to be represented on high-visibility technical projects, they were also less likely to be seen as having the skill set most valued by leaders. And because women were less likely to be seen as possessing those technical skills, they were less likely to be picked for highly visible groups. For example, women were not always invited to contribute to "blue sky" teams, the groups that companies ask to do the biggest, boldest thinking about new technologies and businesses. As one male manager explained, these high-visibility opportunities were not offered to everyone: "People get handpicked by senior folks to think about this stuff."

The same pattern happened with leadership skills. During performance reviews, we found that the highest marks were given to employees who fit a narrow definition of leadership that tended to reflect a highly visible style. Terms such as “crushes it” and “kills it” were used to describe top performers. But while highly visible behaviors benefited senior men, senior women were often criticized when exhibiting them. Comments such as “She is abrasive and runs over people” were given to women. Because women are more likely to be described as having a collaborative, less visible leadership style, they were less likely to win recognition within these narrow definitions.

## Visibility in Assignments

In order to advance women, companies should focus less on mentorship programs and more on putting women into stretch assignments that build both skills and organizational visibility.[3]

Our research suggests that women are less able to access these assignments. Some of the women in our focus groups described being turned away when they requested big, new opportunities. One explained, “There are times where you are discouraged from taking on a stretch assignment. The manager says, ‘This will require extra hours, and you have to think about your family. This is not something for you.’ I have had that happen to me, and these were experiences needed for a promotion.”

Women also commented on how their likability affected their ability to land choice assignments. They recognized that a penalty could come from being perceived as too aggressive at work. "A lot of characteristics for the men are seen as assets but are not liked in women," said one focus group participant. For example, "He is a driver; she is demanding and bossy. He is quick; she is agitated."

## Visibility in Networks

In addition to being visible for the right skills and the right projects, employees also need to be visible to the right people if they want to advance into senior leadership. In one company where we analyzed a sample of performance evaluations, women were half as likely to be talked about in terms of being known to leaders, and twice as likely to be told they needed to increase their visibility to leadership. Having a leader as a sponsor was one of the few factors in our analysis that did support women achieving high ratings, while having the technical skills alone did not.[4]

Because we tend to network more easily with those we perceive as being similar to us, and because women are underrepresented in positions of power, women are less likely to have the network connections with high-visibility leaders that lead to promotion. One senior woman who *was* highly visible called these connections the "secret sauce of promotions" and said that they are built over informal networks: "There is a little club that goes out drinking, and there is a poker group where women don't get invited. A lot of decision making happens there." Another woman noted, "In one of my reviews, I received written feedback: 'She needs to network more with visible leaders.' Verbally, I was told it means, 'You need to go have drinks with [this person].'"

## Closing the Visibility Gap

How can companies ensure women and men have equal opportunities to build their visibility (and promotability) within the organization? We suggest these steps:

- **Question what is valued.** Examine your promotion criteria and ask: "Are we defining leadership too narrowly and according to an aggressive management style?"
- **Equalize access to assignments.** Bring more awareness and transparency around the allocation of high-visibility stretch assignments.
- **Open up networks.** Create more opportunities for women to connect with senior leaders through high-visibility working groups, Q&A sessions, and inclusive networking events.

By clarifying criteria, making the promotion process more transparent, distributing meaningful assignments equitably, and opening up the right networks for women, we can keep women in tech and build a diverse, talented cohort of leaders.

*Adapted from "To Succeed in Tech, Women Need More Visibility," on hbr.org, September 13, 2016 (product #H034AG).*

SECTION TWO

# Stop Competing, Start Connecting

# 3

# When Women Compete

A conversation with Leah Sheppard

People often think of competition as a healthy part of work. But that's not always true when the competition is among women. Whether we're vying for a major promotion, trying to earn a bigger bonus, or maneuvering to get our way on an important decision, people who see us arguing for what we want might not view it favorably if we're going up against a female colleague. And for the women involved, it can make a friendly competition or growth opportunity feel like intense conflict.

In this conversation, *Women at Work* cohosts Amy Bernstein, Amy Gallo, and Nicole Torres talk to Leah Sheppard, an associate professor in the Carson College of Business at Washington State University, about the nature of competition at work and how to keep our disagreements—and people's perceptions of them—from getting personal.

AMY BERNSTEIN: I want to start with the negative narrative about women in competition at work. What do you know about that?

LEAH SHEPPARD: There is this negative narrative that women have problematic relationships with other women at work or that they're uniquely competitive with one another. Then when we see *any* type of competition occurring among women—even though it's normal between human beings—we interpret it in light of this negative stereotype.

I have research showing that the exact same conflict scenario is viewed differently in terms of how problematic it's going to be. Observers assume that when two women are having the conflict, it's going to take longer to resolve, these individuals are going to be more affected by it, and their job satisfaction and job performance could suffer as a result.

So we do tend to think that there are more negative implications stemming from a conflict scenario when two women are involved as opposed to two men or a man and a woman.

AMY B.: What do you think is behind this?

LEAH: Competition between women violates what we call "prescriptive stereotypes," stereotypes that prescribe certain behavior for women. First, in terms of individual women, we already prescribe certain behavior for them: We want to see warm and nurturing behavior. Then when we think about women's relationships, that carries over: We want to see warm, supportive behaviors occurring within those relationships.

There might be an additional prescription there, because we think of women as being somewhat disadvantaged in the workforce. They don't tend to reach high-ranking leadership roles with the same frequency that men do, and there is a pay gap. We also want to see that women are constantly supporting one another, that they're lifting one another up. So if we do see some normal competition and conflict, it violates that prescriptive stereotype and we react negatively.

AMY B.: This is dangerous, right?

LEAH: Yes. It's taking something that's normal and even healthy and making it problematic. Also, it's somewhat of a double standard because we expect men to be competing with one another; we normalize that. That's OK.

It's dangerous because in some ways it's shifting the responsibility for this gender inequity that we see at work to women themselves. It's saying, *Well, once women reach high-ranking leadership roles, they should be pulling other women up behind them.* And if they're not actively doing that, then they're somehow responsible for any inequality that we see.

**NICOLE TORRES:** How do women compete with each other at work? Does it look different from how we might compete with men?

**LEAH:** I don't know that it would be different, honestly. Anytime you have scarce resources, as you do in organizations—only certain people might be able to get certain roles, everyone can't have a leadership position, everyone can't have the highest salary—you're going to see similar types of behaviors emerge. What's salient about it is where it's occurring. There are women who are generally competing with other women at work because they see those women as being the most similar to them and therefore their most likely competitors.

Again, though, it goes back to these gender stereotypes. Women might feel a bit more comfortable competing against a man because they think, *Well, for him it's normal, he's used to it. I can be a little bit ferocious against him and it's OK.* They might feel somewhat more reserved when they're competing against another woman.

**NICOLE:** I have a male colleague here, and we have a lot of friendly competitions—who can do more editing in a month or something. But when I thought about it, I don't have friendly competitions with other women. I kind of avoid those. That might speak to what you're talking about.

**LEAH:** Is it that you avoid the competition altogether or that it somehow feels more toxic when it does happen?

**NICOLE:** It's a little more uncomfortable. I feel like it's something we avoid. When I'm talking to female friends, like if we're playing a game, we're fighting over who didn't win—*You won that one.* We're just complimenting each other and we're not as competitive. But with male colleagues or male friends, it is just a more friendly competition.

**LEAH:** That probably goes back to some of the prescriptions around what you *should* be doing, how you *should* be behaving in those relationships. We always hear people cheering on women supporting other women. And I'm sure that spills over into our friendships, where we think, *Oh, I don't want to actively criticize someone or compete with them. Even if it's all in good fun, I might be viewed as being unsupportive or being catty.*

**NICOLE:** What's the impact of that, though?

**LEAH:** It could just reinforce the stereotype. If we did see more of this behavior, especially all in good fun, it might normalize women's competition, and perhaps that could change the stereotypes. (See the sidebar, "Break the Cycle of Female Rivalry.")

## Break the Cycle of Female Rivalry

BY MIKAELA KINER

Most women invite and value *healthy* competition—fighting fairly for a job, project, or promotion. But a big driver of female rivalry is the concept of "one seat at the table." When women adopt this mindset and fight among themselves, it holds all women back.

If a woman wants to get ahead, the better course is to champion the women around her, resulting in more opportunities and increased success for all. Here are some ways to do just that.

- **Help women through mentorship, advocacy, and creating opportunities.** You can redefine how women interact at work by proving there's room for many to succeed. If you see a woman struggling, don't judge her—ask how you can help. Share information about how you've succeeded on projects and how you've effectively built relationships.

- **Amplify other women's ideas and suggestions.** Doing so in meetings, for example, increases their chance of being heard. If a woman is interrupted in a meeting, ask her to finish her thought. That way, she gets the floor and you didn't have to call anyone out.

- **Give women credit for their ideas, contributions, and accomplishments.** Publicly praise women who do well—in meetings, over email, and even in casual settings.
- **Share your skills and knowledge.** If you have a skill that's in high demand, host a brown bag lunch and invite other women to join you. If that feels like too much work, start a book group where women can get to know each other and build relationships. The informal friendships that women build will serve them well in the more formal work setting.
- **Collectively ask for what you need at work.** Partnering with other women is a proven way to influence leaders and effect change. Join your company's employee resource group, and use it to discuss issues that affect women and brainstorm solutions to share with your sponsor. If your company doesn't have a forum for women, start one yourself.
- **Do not talk badly about other women.** Doing so doesn't help anyone, especially if it's gossip or throwing someone under the bus. If you have constructive feedback for another woman, share it with her directly and respectfully. Talk *to* her, not *about* her.

*(continued)*

- **Don't let sexist jokes or comments go.** Even a phrase like "I didn't find that funny" or "What did you mean by that?" disrupts inappropriate behavior. And it's so much easier to do this when the comment isn't directed at you.
- **Raise issues that affect women, and encourage others to do the same.** Company suggestion boxes and leadership Q&A sessions can be good venues for this. I worked at one company where an anonymous question about insufficient maternity leave led to a complete overhaul and much more generous time off for mothers.
- **Stop expecting more from women than from men.** Don't judge women, including yourself, with a double standard. Assume best intentions, and if someone's behavior doesn't make sense to you, get curious and find out more.
- **Learn from those who have been working longer than you.** Reach out to your more experienced female peers and talk to them about the battles they've faced and what they've had to overcome. They will appreciate your asking.

Adapted from "It's Time to Break the Cycle of Female Rivalry," Ascend, on hbr.org, April 14, 2020.

If women are holding themselves back from that, if they don't want to be perceived that way, it could have career impacts. If you've never put yourself into the competition for something at work, where does your career go from there? You might see some career stalling, that's one side of it. The other side would be that this stereotype just keeps getting reinforced.

**AMY GALLO:** When there are only two, three, or five women in an organization, does that mean you get pitted against one another more often?

**LEAH:** There is some research to support that. Especially if women are looking to the top of the organization and are seeing very few spots available to women, they're then going to think, *OK, only one of us can make it to the top*. Robin Ely at Harvard Business School interviewed women working in law firms with either zero or a few female partners, and she noted that the relationships among the female lawyers who were not in those senior roles yet were more strained and competitive when there were fewer women at the top. So yes, scarcity could absolutely play in here.

Unfortunately, there are not as many contexts in which you can see whether the same thing happens with men when they're outnumbered, especially at the top of the organization. Because that's what is really driving the effects. It's not so much just being outnumbered at any given level of the workforce; it's when you're looking at leadership roles and the representation of women and men in those roles. Unfortunately, it's hard to find industries where the women reliably outnumber the men in top leadership. But it would be interesting to see how that would affect men's feelings of competitiveness or conflict with one another.

NICOLE: What kinds of behavior from a woman might make other women think that she's trying to compete with them?

LEAH: Probably a woman's agentic behavior—things that we might ascribe more to men, like being ambitious, dominant, asserting oneself, promoting oneself and one's accomplishments, and being independent in how you work. We know from research that anytime a woman adopts behavior that is somewhat more masculine, there can be a backlash effect against that. She might be seen as being very agentic and even highly competent because she's behaving in a way that's consistent with that—but we might also see her as being somewhat cold and unlikable. That kind of behavior could ruffle some feathers, and that could happen among both female and male observers. If she's somewhat unapologetic about seeking power, that would be the ambition component, which could make both men and women feel threatened.

AMY B.: It sounds as if we frequently confuse competition with interpersonal problems. How do we separate those?

LEAH: If we think about the definition of these behaviors, they all fall within conflict scenarios, because even if there's competition and it's not personal, I'm fighting for my interests and they might come at the expense of yours. So, at least in my academic brain, we would still define that as a conflict. But academics also talk a lot about healthy forms of conflict. When conflict is about the task at hand, for example, we would think that that's a healthy kind of conflict that could actually lead to better outcomes, as long as it's a moderate amount.

In terms of just managing the impressions around these things, there's a couple of ways that we can go about this. If you're in a competition and don't want to be interpreted negatively, have a conversation with the other person. Make sure they're evaluating what's happening in the same way you are, that they're not feeling as though there's an interpersonal conflict here that is really just healthy competition. You might be having fun with it and enjoying yourself. Are they? Are they experiencing it in the same way?

It's also important how you talk about that situation among other people. Are you giving the impression that there is some interpersonal hostility here? That would probably be the case if you were gossiping about that person or talking about them behind their back.

But if your colleagues and other observers are the ones coming to you and trying to talk about it or get you to gossip, don't fall into that trap. You want to be very careful in how you respond, and you should probably say explicitly, "It's really no big deal and you're making it overly dramatic." Maybe shift it to them a little bit and make them feel a little bit silly for dramatizing something that doesn't need to be dramatized. Reassure them that this really was just about the task at hand and there's nothing personal going on.

AMY G.: I think we forget when we have conflicts or compete with others at work that there are observers that are going to both interpret for you what's going on and then either reinforce or change that narrative. I talk sometimes about the emotional shrapnel of a conflict, where everyone else experiences the aftereffects of your conflict. You have to manage those aftereffects so that they don't reinforce or reignite the conflict that you've already had.

LEAH: Exactly. That can be a really stressful component: What are other people thinking about this? Are they then going to the other party and speaking to them and changing their narrative as well? It's all part of our sense-making process. We absolutely talk these things through with other people, and it all becomes part of our perceptions of the event.

AMY G.: I take from what you're saying that (1) we have to think about managing the perception with others. So, rather than saying, "You know how I feel about Nicole," you can say, "Nicole and I are having a healthy debate about this and we're working together to find a solution."

But then (2) if you feel a woman is trying to undermine you, you should check your gender bias. Right?

**LEAH:** Right.

**AMY G.:** If we overestimate that negativity, how can we as women stop doing that, to lessen that interpretation?

**LEAH:** Well, it's exactly what you said—checking our biases: How do I feel about the situation? Do I have these suspicions about this other woman for valid reasons? Let me think about what's happened so far. Has anyone else reacted this way to me? Have men done the same thing? Am I interpreting this differently because it involves another woman?

It's always interesting to me because in doing this research and then having conversations about it, people are always fascinated by this topic. Sometimes you'll come across women who will say things like, "Yeah, anytime I've had problems with someone at work, it's been a woman" or "Yeah, I don't get along with women." Then if you probe a little bit and ask, "Can you think of times when you've not gotten along with men?" or "Who are your closest friends at work?" you'll find out that they *have* had conflicts with men. Or they'll say, "Well, yes, all my closest friends at work are women." It's trying to make the person aware of the contradictions in their stories, that they're saying one thing but when they analyze it deeper or you ask them follow-up questions, they say something completely different.

That's something else we can do, not only with ourselves but with other people too. When we hear others spreading this narrative, probe a little bit and ask some follow-up questions. That could help them interpret this in a different light and go, "Yeah, maybe the stories of my conflict with women are somehow more salient to me than the conflicts that I've experienced with men." That could go a long way.

I'm always amazed at people's willingness to perpetuate these stereotypes, because they don't reflect well on anyone. If a woman is saying, "I don't work well with other women" or "Other women don't work well with me," that's basically just saying the problem is us. We're tearing down our own group in some ways by perpetuating that.

So I'm not saying that women shouldn't talk about these things or that they should be silenced; obviously, we want to talk about these things because it's healthy to do so. But try to represent them fairly in our minds and in how we describe them. Try to consider the other side about how we have felt in our relationships and conflicts with men—and what kinds of conflicts we observe between men at work as well. Do we focus on those things, or do we just normalize them and push them to the side?

*Adapted from "When Women Compete,"* Women at Work *podcast season 3, episode 6, May 20, 2019.*

# 4

# Building Relationships When You Feel Excluded

by Brenda F. Wensil and Kathryn Heath

A male friend of ours, Will, had a realization. He was walking through the bar at a private golf club, looking for a colleague he was meeting for dinner. The dark-paneled bar was filled with men who all seemed to know each other. Will wasn't a member of the club, and he felt a little out of place. When he found his friend and they sat down at a table, he felt more comfortable. Then he looked around and realized that only about five of the 35 people in the large room were women. Even if they were members, these women stood out in this mostly male setting. He could blend in so easily. These women didn't have that luxury.

Welcome to our world. As female executives, it's sometimes difficult for us to fit in, but we need to be in that room nonetheless.

There are typically two ways to get things done professionally. One way is explicit, established, and formalized: the job-specific mode we use to accomplish our work every day. Job descriptions, agenda items, expertise, and hierarchy dictate how this work is done and how formal decisions are made. The other way is informal, highly nuanced, and relationship-based. It involves leveraging human connections, corporate maneuvering, physical proximity to decision makers, and personal and professional influence inside the office and outside at informal gatherings.

While both ways are important, we have seen in our work coaching women executives that they overwhelmingly struggle more than men to take advantage of informal networking situations. Part of the problem is systemic: When men go out together after work, women often are not invited. Eighty-one percent of women say they feel this type of social exclusion in work situations.[1] Based on published reports, this problem has further intensified since #MeToo, with men saying that they feel more hesitant to socialize with female colleagues for fear that their motives might be called into question.[2]

The other issue is that some women often can't or don't want to socialize after work or during work hours. They keep their heads down at the office to maximize their efforts, and then they feel pressure to head home to spend time with their families (and often to start their "night shift" of cooking, laundry, homework help, and bedtime routines). Many of our women coaching clients have told us things like: *I don't have time to go out with the group. Nothing gets done at these things anyway. It's all politics.*

Regardless of the rationale, the effect is the same: Doing less relationship building limits women's access to sponsorship and diminishes their chances for career advancement. Developing informal relationships is one of the most important things women can do to advance their careers. With our livelihoods on the line, we need to turn this dynamic around.

By committing to a manageable combination of informal relationship building inside and outside the office, we can amplify our efforts and develop genuine influence with senior colleagues and decision makers. Here's how.

## Leverage informal norms

Is your workplace a coffee culture? Do people play cards or grab a drink together after hours? Knowing what social rituals define your organization makes relationships easier to manage. There's no need to get a lunch on the calendar, for instance, if you know the executive vice president is in line at Starbucks every morning at 7 a.m. Regardless of the specifics, seize easy opportunities to connect.

Similarly, examine the cross-silo social networks that underlie your organization. Perhaps the tech-savvy crowd sits together at staff meetings, or the young moms meet at the park on Sundays. Even if you don't fit within any of the social networks yourself, just knowing who does can tell you who's closely connected to whom. This also applies to the social networking tools that people use. Knowing how people connect allows you to reach out to them more easily.

## Make meaningless time more meaningful

Legitimate time constraints are the most common reason women cite for ditching dinner with colleagues or skipping "optional" work events. Because of that, it's crucial to maximize the time we do have. For instance, arrive five minutes early to meetings and start a conversation, or walk to the train with someone who's going your way. An accomplished publishing executive we coach arrives to the office 10 minutes early every morning and walks around the building. Sometimes she has an agenda; other times she simply stops to chat with whoever's milling around. She always catches somebody and finds out what's going on. If she's proposing a new project at the following week's meeting, she gets early feedback and she's more prepared for her presentation. The point is to make your extraneous time more meaningful by using it to form connections. The informal information flow is powerful.

## Suit yourself

Relationship building is never a one-size-fits-all proposition. Don't bother learning to play tennis if that's not your thing. Decide what you like—opera, ball games, wine tasting, trendy eateries—and invite a few colleagues along for fun. If you are an introvert, don't go it alone. Meet a few work friends and head to the company party with them; it's fine to work the room in pairs. The same goes for informal socializing: It doesn't need to be a one-on-one event. Getting a group together to have drinks or dinner makes it easier to talk to someone you don't know. Many women also prefer to invite colleagues and their spouses or partners into their home, instead of meeting solo or going out to dinner together.

Doing it the way you want to makes you more comfortable and lets people get to know you in a way that can change how they perceive you.

## Face forward

It's not only teenagers who can't tear their eyes away from their smartphones; screens rob all of us of precious face-to-face interactions. This is an easy one: Stop hiding behind your phone. Look people in the eye and talk to them, whether it's before the meeting starts, on your way to lunch, on the stairs, or in the elevator. Simply being fully present will help you make many more crucial connections.

As women, we need to continue to work together to think of new solutions to this old problem. The higher we rise in organizations, the more important informal interactions become. Regardless of the venue or activity, relationship building is just another part of the job.

*Adapted from "4 Ways Women Can Build Relationships When They Feel Excluded at Work," on hbr.org, July 27, 2018 (product #H04GN5).*

# 5

# Sponsorship Is Support

## A conversation with Cristina Massa and Julia González Romero

To get ahead at work, we need support from people besides our boss. Sometimes that comes in the form of mentorship, where a person with more experience gives us advice or guidance on how we can improve. But there is another kind of support that is equally if not more important: sponsorship, where someone with a lot of power in the company advocates on our behalf.

In this conversation with *Women at Work* cohost Amy Bernstein, we learn how two women, Cristina Massa and Julia González Romero, who work at a law firm in Mexico City, approach their sponsorship relationship to see what other women can learn from them.

AMY BERNSTEIN: Cristina, what was it that you saw in Julia that made you want to invest in her?

**CRISTINA MASSA:** I've seen her work, even in those positions in the federal government where I did not manage or supervise her in any way. She was well known and regarded for being very hardworking, intelligent, and brave. She tackled all her jobs, studying technically and seeking advice. That's not something we see all the time.

**AMY:** Is the sponsor-protégé relationship that you two have something you've discussed, or has it simply evolved organically?

**CRISTINA:** Some parts have been implicit, but others we have discussed. In this firm, we have 20 partners—19 male partners and myself as a female partner—so I'm acutely aware of some of the gender issues that we face. I am also a mother. Some of the specific challenges for women, both professionally and personally, are around how to devote substantial resources to both aspects of yourself. Sometimes you're just sort of trying to manage it all, and it's hard to reach out to someone for help and say, "I don't know how this works. I don't know where to get the money or the resources or the plane tickets" or whatever it is. It doesn't have to be anything very big. It can be something as trivial as asking for the resources you need to do your job.

I knew that if I didn't help Julia out, it would be much harder for her. But she also came forward to ask the right questions: "I want to go to this event. I don't know how to do it. How can I get the support to do this? How can I ask to see this senior partner and tell him what I do? Do I just walk in? Do I need to make an appointment? Do I need to make a call?" She didn't know how to do that, but she knew that she could ask. I've tried to do my part.

**AMY:** Julia, how do you see it?

**JULIA GONZÁLEZ ROMERO:** The first week I was in the law firm, Cristina was traveling. I've been working for 17 years, and I felt lost because I didn't know the rules of engagement. So when Cristina came back from her trip, the first thing I did was ask her about everything I didn't understand, which was most of how the law firm works, because this is a completely different environment than what I'm used to. But Cristina has gone further, because she saw that I was struggling in certain areas, and she made sure I met with the right people so I could have the exposure I needed to move forward.

**AMY:** Cristina, do you remember the moment when you decided to sponsor Julia?

**CRISTINA:** Yes. We both have a government background, and I heard very early on after she was hired that she was seen as one of the "government implants" that don't really know how to talk the talk. I got a call from another partner saying, "I hear that we've got one of these government people in the environmental and social impact area. Did you have anything to do with it?" And I said, "Yes, I did. And I'm going to take care of it."

It's not simply altruistic. Since I introduced her to the law firm, Julia's mistakes are also my mistakes. If she doesn't make it here, it's on me as well. All senior women that come to the firm are seen as potential time bombs—they're not going to work that hard because they have kids, they are not going to be as committed, they are not going to bring in that much business. So even if she doesn't work in the antitrust area, I knew that people were watching.

There's this part in which I want to help her, but there's also this part where my position in the firm requires not only that I be a good antitrust expert but also that I build within the firm. That means bringing in talent, and women can be riskier hires than men, just because of the way things work.

**AMY:** What are some examples of the kinds of support that you've given to Julia to help her advance her career?

**CRISTINA:** She happens to work in a practice area that is led by a very traditional partner. He is the oldest person in the firm, and he developed his career in a very traditional way. I knew that she was going to need help there. Those are very vertical relationships where women and junior associates are not expected to go out and sell, invite people, participate in events, and be speakers or teachers without their boss's explicit consent. But then you ask for consent, and they tend to say, "No, I need you to be at the firm, because I am the one that's going to be speaking at this event or taking this trip, and you need to cover my back."

I have been actively pushing for Julia to go to events unaccompanied and unchaperoned. She is the expert on her topic, not her boss. She is a more renowned expert in her matters than her boss. I've had to answer questions of "Where is Julia?" and "Why is she there?"

**JULIA:** I didn't know that.

**CRISTINA:** It does come up. "Why does she go places without going through the proper channels?" And I've said that the proper channel for a grown woman with expertise is going.

**AMY:** We've talked a lot on the podcast about pay transparency and the gender wage gap, and the importance of sponsors discussing compensation with their protégés. Has that conversation taken place between you two?

**CRISTINA:** It did. We don't have lockstep compensation—it's every person for themselves negotiating salary. Before Julia told me the number, I told her, "They're going to expect to pay less because you're a woman, and they are going to expect you not to negotiate hard, because good girls don't do that." Women are "nice"; they graciously accept whatever they are offered, and they are thankful that they have a job, even if they have kids, husbands, households, or anything else to take care of. So I told Julia, "Don't let them pull that card on you. I'm not part of your compensation committee because you're in another practice area. I will not be able to take care of you. You need to do that yourself. But you really need to play hardball."

I take part in some other negotiations, and I see the incredible difference in men and women negotiating their salaries, so I knew that that was going to be an issue.

**JULIA:** Which it wasn't, because I played hardball, thanks to Cristina.

**CRISTINA:** She has one of the highest compensations in the firm, I have to say.

**AMY:** That is fantastic.

**JULIA:** Thanks to Cristina.

**CRISTINA:** She deserves it. She has a very senior position. This was not a gracious concession. Typically, they would have said, "Maybe you will need flexibility because of your kids" and that type of thing. They would have pressed hard.

**AMY:** Cristina, what do you get out of this relationship? How does this benefit you?

**CRISTINA:** Bringing in talent gives me standing in the firm. People that work with Julia are going to be very happy with her job. As people get more senior, they also start bringing in business. My biggest challenge at the firm is to keep a flow of work coming in, so I know that in every pitch that Julia gives, she's going to promote the antitrust area. I will be very mad if she doesn't. [*Laughter*] If her clients bring their antitrust business anywhere else, I will resent it. I am expecting those clients to come in from her.

There are a few other female associates that are doing an incredibly good job, and I've spent substantial time to make sure that Julia hangs out with them, that she participates in initiatives with them, because being the sole female partner and not having a pipeline of powerful women—it's a queen bee scenario that I don't want in my firm, where I made it and I don't care if anybody else does. That is terrible for the firm, and it's also bad for me.

Julia also has great connections. She's a good person to have on your side. And I like her, too.

**AMY:** Julia, are you aware when Cristina has thrown her influence behind an opportunity when it's presented to you?

**JULIA:** Sometimes I am, sometimes I'm not. For example, I have the support of another senior partner, and I know that Cristina has talked to him because he told me: "Cristina spoke to me and told me you're one of the most talented girls she's worked with. And I'm going to bat for you, because she's betting on you." But I didn't know that she has to account for the time I'm out selling, though, because I'm a good seller.

**AMY:** Do you tell Julia when you are fighting on her behalf for something?

**CRISTINA:** Sometimes I don't. I haven't told her some of the questions that arise or when there is a bit of conflict about her time and how she devotes it. When it is relevant—because I know that it's going to get back to her—I tell her. When I think she's not going to hear about it and it's not relevant for her to know or it's housekeeping matters, I don't tell her. I don't want her to feel more stressed.

In law firms, it's all about generating work and getting the work done. If in the end everything works out fine and she ends up landing the account or providing an excellent service to her client, nobody's going to remember the little bending of the rules that I pushed. I tell her when I think it's going to get back to her one way or the other.

**AMY:** Do you guys ever have conflict in your relationship?

**CRISTINA:** Well, sometimes Julia can be a bit intense with the help that she needs or the questions she wants answered. Sometimes they require late-night calls, or early-morning messages, or—

**JULIA:** Both.

**CRISTINA:** Or she'll show up in my office unannounced and speak very quickly about nine things that are concerning her. And sometimes I say, "I do not have time for this right now. I know you expect help, but I can't do it right now." Or, "I know you want to push this, but here you would not be bending the rules. You would be breaking them, and I cannot help you do that. These are my partners. I can push it this hard, but I cannot push it *that* hard. It's too costly for you, and it's costly for me. So I don't think this is worth it."

I'm not sure that I've been right every time. But she's been a very good sport about it. But sometimes I tell her, "You need to drop this issue. I know that it is bothering you. I know you want to raise it. I know you want to talk about it. But let's go have a drink and talk about it, you and me. You're not going to talk to my partners about this. Let's just tough it out."

I wouldn't call it conflict, because she's been good about taking that advice. But one of these days, she's going to say, "I don't know, I really want to fight this." Then maybe some conflict will arise. But I think that we're ready for it. Bring it on, Julia.

**AMY:** Julia, do you ever feel at odds with Cristina?

**JULIA:** No, because I see Cristina as someone who's helping me. I do know I can be too strong. Cristina helps me with my boundaries. I know if Cristina's telling me no, I need to stop. She's a reality check.

**AMY:** Cristina, you have invested an awful lot of your time, effort, and social capital in Julia. Do you have other protégés?

**CRISTINA:** I do. I don't think they have been as intense as Julia, but there are a few other associates that I work closely with to help them advance their careers and provide the type of services that I think will be best for our firm going forward. I try to work particularly hard with female associates, but some of our rising stars are men, and I work hard with them as well in explaining some of the rules, helping them with all these implicit assumptions that have taken me six years at the firm to learn. But I do believe almost everything that I've done in my career has been because I had mentors and sponsors myself.

When I was at the beginning of my career, one of my biggest sponsors strongly recommended that I get a graduate degree in the United States—and this was more than 20 years ago. It was not viewed well. My family did not support the idea of me living abroad alone. I did not have economic support, even to explore the idea of a foreign degree. This sponsor paid for my applications, for my exams, and even for a trip for me to go interview at law schools in the States. I saw the difference that support can make.

In that instance it was financial, but it was not only that. The sponsor spoke to my parents. I was an adult, but in Mexico that was the way things worked. He called my parents and explained why he believed I needed to get this degree. My father thought that I should get my admission letter to Harvard, frame it, and hang it in my bedroom but never go. My sponsor convinced my father to allow me to go. That was the sort of influence that somebody had on me at the time.

I haven't done anything as generous as paying for someone's applications, exams, and travels. But I have always tried to at least recognize the power that those things can have in someone and give it back.

**AMY:** So you have been both a protégé and a sponsor. What would you say to someone who's looking for a sponsor like you?

**CRISTINA:** You have to be proactive. You cannot wait for people to take care of you. You need to reach out, ask questions, and don't take it hard when they say, "I can't do it right now."

What I've seen in mentorship programs is that they fail not because of lack of interest from the mentors, but because of lack of proactivity from the mentees. Women in particular, when they are young, they have not faced discrimination at all. In law school, it's been half and half since I can remember. When I went to school, we were already 50/50, and women didn't have to struggle to get a job.

It gets harder as you get more senior and you're expected to do a lot of things that you're not prepared to do, or when you have a family. Younger women are not necessarily that proactive. Because Julia came to the firm as a lateral and she already had three kids, she had to make it work. Her income is important; her work-life balance is not a question of "if." She just has to do it, so she has all the motivation. Younger associates that are not facing such an unsurmountable pile of problems are not as proactive. They expect you to take them out, to take care of them, to explain where to turn on the light.

So that's what I would recommend. Keep a close tab on your mentor or sponsor.

**AMY:** Any final thoughts from you, Julia?

**JULIA:** I've been lucky to have many sponsors throughout my life, and I believe that has shaped my career. But as Cristina says, I look to her for help as much as I do because I know no one's going to help me unless I ask.

*Adapted from "Sponsorship: Defining the Relationship,"* Women at Work *podcast season 4, episode 3, October 29, 2019.*

# 6

# Identifying Male Allies in Your Organization

by Tsedale M. Melaku and Christoph Winkler

Women have faced significant obstacles in attempting to climb the ranks in the workplace. The journey continues to be fraught with structural barriers that prevent them from gaining access to the same level of opportunities enjoyed by most men—from confidence hurdles, mommy-track narratives, boys' clubs, and exclusion from professional and social networking to heightened barriers resulting from #MeToo, Covid-19, and racial violence.[1] Women continue to struggle to find the support and advocacy they need and identify the allies who can help them.

Allyship is defined as a strategic mechanism used intentionally by individuals who strive to be *collaborators*, *accomplices*, and *coconspirators*. Allies are deeply invested in challenging and disrupting the status quo, dismantling systemic inequities, and shifting the power structure within an organization. Allyship is a practice that needs to be embedded within an individual's sense of everyday commitment to equity. Thus, an ally must be invested in the larger goals of fighting for equity and be accountable for their actions.

An ally's behavior often works to reduce the amount of invisible labor expended by marginalized individuals in white-male-dominated organizations.[2] Allies work publicly and privately to change workplace practices, cultures, and policies that negatively impact marginalized groups. By building authentic and trusting relationships, engaging in public advocacy and sponsorship, and fighting injustice, allies help to create equitable professional and social spaces by strategically deploying their privilege in support of those less privileged.

Anyone and everyone can be an ally. But male allies who recognize and understand the importance of fostering an inclusive, welcoming, and equitable workplace culture can help break down the barriers that women face at work.

Since men often hold powerful positions in organizations (particularly in male-dominated fields), women can work with these allies to dismantle the systemic power structures that prevent equal opportunity for professional development and advancement—for themselves and the other women around them. Only then will women and other marginalized groups have the ability to fully contribute as equally valued employees toward an ever-evolving organization's mission and values.

But how can women identify male allies in the workplace? In the following, we provide a guide to spotting a male ally.

## Take the Temperature

First, take the temperature of your organization. Scan the environment for clear indicators of growth and opportunity. Ask yourself:

- Do you see people from underrepresented groups advancing to leadership positions, or does the organization have a portfolio of diversity with high attrition and no clear path upward?
- Are there embedded practices and policies that address issues stemming from gender, racial, and other inequities?

It is easier to chart a pathway toward people who are genuine allies if you have seen them help marginalized group members advance, particularly women of color. Typically, it's a red flag if you're not seeing any indications that members of an underrepresented group are offered opportunities for growth. These observations could potentially be a sign of a weak culture of allyship, among other workplace equity concerns within the organization.

## Look for Patterns

Pay attention to details. Actively seek out the individuals you recognize as practicing allyship. See how these individuals position marginalized individuals in public meetings, paying attention to what they are saying when they are silent or how they respond in pressured situations that challenge various forms of privilege. Allies step in when they recognize that something is wrong, whether it is an aggression, discrimination, or an unfair practice. They do not leave their marginalized colleagues feeling as though they are alone.

Ask yourself these questions when trying to identify an ally:

- Does this person speak up in pressured moments, exercising their voice and deploying their privilege to point out inequities?
- Do their actions match their words? Do their public displays of support add up to concrete results?
- Are there people who have a genuine interest in helping marginalized individuals advance? If so, who are these people?

For example, Black women are often stereotyped as angry, confrontational, or sensitive when they step up to address racial aggressions, making it difficult for them to be heard.[3] Allies can do the heavy lifting in these moments, ensuring that their colleagues are not forced to expend emotional, cognitive, and relational labor to navigate fraught situations.[4] (See the sidebar, "A Call to Women.") Allies actively listen, following the lead of marginalized colleagues they are supporting to avoid eliciting further pain or trauma. This means working toward building equity by educating themselves; directing attention to inequities without silencing those who are marginalized; being kind, thoughtful, and open to disagreements; and learning and admitting their mistakes.

## Beware of Performative Allyship

We know that authentic allyship comes with a genuine attempt, where those who have privilege deploy it to advocate publicly and privately for those who are marginalized—or just to do the right thing—without promoting one's virtuousness. And allies do this to effect change.

Performative allyship is the opposite, where individuals label themselves allies and profess to be in solidarity with gender, racial, or any other type of equity project without committing to doing the work or even believing in its necessity. They do this to strategically limit scrutiny of their actions. Often they perform surface-level work—gestures, statements, or even social media posts—for personal gain or to make an impression on others without any intention of tackling structural issues or making a change.[5] Performative allyship maintains the status quo and delegitimizes the work that needs to be done to address systemic and structural barriers that sustain all forms of inequity.[6]

Actions speak louder than words. If you're not seeing the results behind someone's claims, you may want to steer clear.

## Trust Your Gut and Take a Chance, But . . .

Once you have identified someone you perceive to be an ally, based on their pattern of behavior and proven efforts, the ball is in your court. The previous suggestions are prerequisites to taking a calculated risk when it comes to building a trusting relationship with someone you think could be an ally. Taking a chance includes being present, developing a rapport, and actively putting in the time to nurture a trusting relationship. However, you must trust your gut and continue to pay attention to how members of the organization are demonstrating a commitment to building and sustaining an equitable workplace through authentic allyship across all company stakeholders.[7] For

## A Call to Women

While the tips we've provided speak generally to the experiences of women and the need to identify male allies, we must also consider the impact of multiple intersecting identities that create nuanced challenges for marginalized individuals, such as Black women.[8] For instance, white women are often beneficiaries of white male allyship, while Black women are not due to the double burden of racial *and* gender oppression, as well as other forms of oppression that intersect, combine, and overlap to create inequities.[9] It is imperative that white women, too, have a shared responsibility to deploy their white privilege to support other marginalized groups. The question then becomes, once women rise, how can they move toward lifting those whom they know are facing similar, if not more, structural barriers in the workplace?

example, have you noticed anyone calling attention to problematic behavior and challenging colleagues to reflect on how their actions go against institutional commitments to equity, or have they remained silent?

Having a true ally in the workplace means knowing not only that you have an accomplice, collaborator, and advocate but also that others will too. An ally is bound by the profound commitment to challenge and dismantle systems of inequality to ensure that everyone is treated equally; has access to professional growth, development, and advancement; and has a safe and equitable place to work. The tips discussed here are a general guide to how you can identify that person. But know that the onus should not just be on women and other marginalized groups. An ally will be revealed through their actions, not their words.

*Adapted from "How Women Can Identify Male Allies in the Workplace," on hbr.org, May 4, 2022 (product #H070ZU).*

SECTION THREE

# Grow Your Confidence

# 7

# Don't Let Self-Doubt Hold You Back

by Alisa Cohn

No matter what job you have or which industry you are in, you need to know which skills and areas to grow in order to progress in your career. Understanding your weaknesses is just as important to your success as recognizing your strengths.

At the same time, this self-awareness must be carefully managed. If you focus too much on your shortcomings and ignore the value you bring to your organization, what started out as productive mindfulness can balloon into insecurity or imposter syndrome, holding you back from reaching your full potential.

As an executive coach, I've worked with a number of professionals who were so focused on their shortcomings that they ended up overwhelmed by self-doubt, unable to take the risks necessary to move forward in their careers.

It's easy to become submerged in your own insecurities—but it is possible to overcome these doubts. Here are four strategies that anyone can use to combat self-doubt and build confidence in the workplace.

## Channel an Alter Ego

Sometimes, being too tuned in to our limitations can make it difficult to move past them. When this happens, it's helpful to gain a little distance from ourselves by channeling an alter ego. Taking on the persona of someone more confident can help you acknowledge the challenges you face without letting them completely take you over. Psychologists call this "self-distancing"—it's a method of gaining perspective that empowers you to get out of your own way and activate more productive behaviors.

For example, one client I worked with, Rebecca (all names have been changed to preserve anonymity), founded a nonprofit to combat homelessness in her community right after graduating from college. Rebecca sometimes had trouble holding her own with the local politicians and, as she described them, the "tough street cops" she had to work with. She told me that she had been raised to respect authority, and so when she met with these politicians and police officers who were so much older and carried such a strong air of authority, she struggled to effectively advocate for her organization.

To help her take charge, I asked her to imagine a character—real or fictional—who she thought would handle these situations in the way she wished that she could. She immediately came up with Anthony Bourdain, the late celebrity chef, who traveled and explored food from all over the world. She told me that for her, Bourdain embodied the kind of fearlessness she wished she had. I encouraged her to channel Bourdain as her alter ego, so right before her next meeting, she took a few moments to imagine how he would approach the interaction. After this short thought exercise, she found that the authority figures seemed less intimidating, enabling her to overcome her insecurities and advocate for herself much more successfully.

## View Yourself Through the Lens of Others

Another strategy that can help snap you out of excessive self-consciousness is to think about yourself from someone else's point of view. This is a technique I used myself when I was just starting out as a coach. One time, while waiting my turn to interview for a prestigious coaching group, I felt myself getting so nervous that my brain started fogging up. I knew I was qualified, and yet I could feel my confidence evaporating by the second.

To escape this spiral of insecurity, I consciously shifted my perspective to think about how my client Chris, a senior vice president at a large technology company, viewed me. Chris intimidated most people, but I had helped him make miraculous strides in his leadership skills, and we had formed a very close relationship. I thought about Chris laughing at me and saying, "What do you have to be nervous about? You're a rock star!" Immediately my anxiety melted away, my mind cleared, and I was able to perform at my best.

## Tune Out Uninformed Feedback

Constructive feedback can be incredibly valuable—but when feedback is not constructive, it's essential to learn to ignore it. Especially if you hold a leadership role or some other visible position within your organization, everyone will have some opinion on how you could do your job better. You have to remember that not everyone's opinion is useful.

This is something that my client Sandy, the head of design at a fashion company, dealt with. Sandy referred to himself as a "very sensitive creator." While his sensitivity was a key part of how he was able to come up with unique, exquisite clothing designs, it also led him to take criticism very personally. Moreover, he was the youngest member of the leadership team, and the other members of the team weren't shy about sharing negative feedback on his designs (even though most of them were about

20 years older than the company's target market). When he was on the receiving end of their input, he would question whether he brought any value to the company at all, destroying his productivity for days.

But when he took a step back and thought about the situation, he could clearly see that this feedback was largely uninformed and unhelpful. To help him distance himself from this irrelevant feedback, I encouraged Sandy to explicitly label these comments as "opinions" and "noise." Instead of reacting so intensely to his colleagues' thoughts, Sandy started to hear the feedback, acknowledge it politely, and recognize what was and wasn't useful. Over time, he became more and more comfortable with noticing and ignoring feedback that was not helpful to him, keeping it from derailing his work and ruining his mood.

## Reframe Your Self-Talk

Whether we realize it or not, we talk to ourselves all the time. This self-talk is mostly unconscious, and it's often highly negative, keeping us stuck in a loop of doubt. (See the sidebar, "Counteracting Stereotype Threat.") Identifying these negative internal voices and intentionally replacing them with a more positive, productive narrative can help get us out of this paralysis and move toward action.

## Counteracting Stereotype Threat

**BY FRANCESCA GINO**

Stereotype threat, or the tendency to "choke" and underperform due to fear of bias, was first documented by psychologist Claude Steele. It often subconsciously creates self-doubt in women, especially in male-dominated spaces.[1] Consider the persistent stereotype that female students are not as strong as males in math and science. In one study, women who were reminded of their gender before taking a math test scored lower than equally qualified men who took the same test.[2] The women's performances suffered because they feared confirming negative female stereotypes.

How can you avoid stereotype threat and overcome these low expectations? The following four actions can help.

**In high-stakes situations, frame your nervous energy as excitement.** This strategy helps reduce anxiety and improves performance. I tried this myself when I taught an executive education team for the first time with male colleagues who were older and more experienced than I was. By focusing on how excited I was about the class and what I could learn from it, I was able to boost my confidence and ended up getting good ratings from the students.

**View stereotyped qualities as pluses rather than minuses.** Research suggests that when women see a stereotypical "feminine" quality like warmth as an *opportunity* instead of a *problem*, they are more resilient and effective as leaders.[3] This requires a simple shift in mindset: what we intentionally decide to focus on as we approach our work.

**Practice breaking the rules.** In a survey of about 500 men and women, most indicated that it is easier for men to break the rules or go against the grain than it is for women.[4] But women can get away with breaking the rules as well.

For instance, after becoming the CEO of WebMD, Patricia Fili-Krushel met with an all-male group of engineers in Silicon Valley. When they asked her what she knew about engineering, she made a zero with her fingers. "However," she said, "I do know how to run businesses, and I'm hoping you can teach me what I need to know about your world."

For good reasons, many female leaders assume they have to be tough as nails and show no weakness. Fili-Krushel broke that rule, and in so doing confounded the engineers' expectations. By being candid and admitting what she didn't know, which the engineers clearly did not expect, Fili-Krushel gained their respect.

*(continued)*

**Make your own rules.** Ava DuVernay is a writer, filmmaker, and television producer. Among her many accomplishments is directing *Selma*, the first film directed by a Black woman to be nominated for the Academy Award for Best Picture.

As a budding filmmaker, DuVernay devoted a lot of time and energy to figuring out how to break into the industry, seeking out people who could advise and support her. Eventually, though, she came to believe that she would be better off making her own films, with her own ideas and budget. "I think there have been cracks made in the glass ceiling by women who can get close enough to hit it," she told *Time* magazine. "But I'm mostly bolstered by folks who create their own ceilings."[5]

Adapted from "4 Ways Women Can Break Barriers by Breaking the Rules," on hbr.org, May 9, 2018 (product #H04BH0).

For instance, Jennifer, a newly promoted partner at a large consulting firm, realized that unhelpful self-talk was getting in her way. When presenting her findings at partner meetings, she would back down whenever she felt even the slightest pushback, keeping her team from seeing the extent of her abilities. The problem was further compounded because this firm had a strong culture of debate, in which lively discussion about ideas was inescapable. To continue advancing, she knew she would have to get comfortable holding her own when challenged in meetings—but she wasn't sure where to start.

To address this self-doubt, we explored why she was so quick to retreat in these situations. Jennifer quickly identified that whenever she was challenged, her inner dialogue immediately went to "I guess I got it wrong." I invited her to choose a more empowering phrase she could use instead, and she came up with "Oh, good, I love a robust discussion." Even though it felt forced at first, Jennifer consciously repeated the new phrase to herself in subsequent meetings. She found that she quickly became more comfortable defending her points even when challenged aggressively, helping her to both feel more confident and make a better impression on her colleagues.

Everyone experiences self-doubt from time to time—and ironically, it's often the most competent and self-aware of us that are the most likely to be distracted by our shortcomings, keeping us from performing as well as we can. There's no curing insecurity entirely (and a healthy dose of humility is a good thing). But with the strategies I've described, you'll be equipped to gain perspective and take the decisive action that you know you're capable of.

*Adapted from content posted on Ascend, hbr.org, February 15, 2021.*

# 8

# Stop Second-Guessing Yourself

by Tucci Ivowi

Once I was in a large auditorium filled with marketing and sales professionals for a training program on the fundamentals of the coffee business. I was a brand manager in a company I had just joined. During the training, someone asked, "What's the difference between soluble coffee and roast and ground coffee?"

It was a simple question. I knew the answer. But I still refrained from raising my hand: What if I was wrong? What if I wound up looking stupid? It was my first day on the job as a new recruit. *It's probably best for someone with more experience to respond*, I thought. I didn't say anything, and someone else used the opportunity to speak up.

Turns out, I had the right answer.

This wasn't a one-off scenario. There have been so many times throughout my career when I've second-guessed my abilities. You know the feeling—that nagging voice in the back of your head, clouding your mind with doubt and insecurity.

Imposter syndrome.

I finally told myself: *You know the answers. You're smart. You have to say something.* I came to realize that even if my answer *was* incorrect, I would learn something new. The benefit of raising my voice outweighed the emotional cost of my silence. I looked at the evidence, and it showed me that no one in my organization had been penalized for getting something wrong. In fact, they had been rewarded for their participation.

After that, I made it a point to contribute. I began to share my point of view, whether or not it differed from the majority perspective. People began to notice. They said I had "leadership potential."

Years later, I joined the senior leadership team of a multinational organization. I was working out of Ghana and heading a business unit for the Central and West African region. At the age of 36, I was the youngest and first African woman to have held that role. I was also the first woman on an otherwise all-male team. Exhilarating as it was, stepping into my new position meant that a number of employees—both men and women—looked up to me as a source of inspiration for what I had achieved and the odds I had beat.

I was already nervous to take on a more senior role, but those feelings were compounded by another truth: I was representing a group of people whose careers may be helped or hindered by my success or failure.

My imposter syndrome snuck back in. *Am I the right person for this job?* I wondered. So I reminded myself that I was there because I was capable. I had to continue doing what I had done throughout my career: focusing on the job, giving it 100%, and delivering results. Nothing more and nothing less.

If you find yourself overtaken by imposter syndrome, I understand. There is probably a myriad of questions going through your head: *Am I really good enough to be doing this? Will I make a fool of myself? Will my colleagues think I'm undeserving of this position?*

Based on my experiences, here are five pieces of advice that can help you dial down the self-criticism and grow in your career, while remaining true to yourself.

## Acknowledge that it's normal to feel nervous

Imposter syndrome is particularly common when you're new or a minority among a group of people that look, behave, or have very different experiences than you. It's normal to feel uncomfortable. In fact, a certain level of nervousness and doubt is good: It counterbalances complacency and can push you to work harder. When I shift my perspective in this way, it helps me get out of my head.

Acknowledging your feelings, but also understanding that they are common, has a way of calming your senses by reducing the angst and reminding you to focus on your goal.

## Don't harbor a fear of failure

The best people can fail, and the most unlikely people can succeed. The unlikely ones are those who fall and get up and try again and again until they finally reach their goal.

Push your fear aside and focus your nervous energy on learning and adding value to your role. Take it one day at a time. When you identify an area of weakness, own it. Think of it as an opportunity to grow. This is how the best leaders gain confidence.

I have always taken personal growth seriously, but I rarely wait around for my organization to send me to workshops or training programs. Most times, the best lessons can be learned at home or on the job.

I read a lot about my areas of business and spend time studying case studies relevant to my work. If you feel you don't have enough information on your industry, read up. If you feel you need to get better in a particular area, ask your employer if they'd be willing to invest in sending you to a course, or sign up for it yourself if you have the resources. If you want to get better at communication skills, practice first in front of family members who can give you honest yet loving feedback, and then in front of colleagues who can give you more technical tips.

Doing this work will grow your confidence—but don't wait until you're perfect to put it into practice. Real learning requires trying and sometimes failing along the way. As ironic as it may sound, failure is one way of refining your craft. You learn everything that can go wrong, and you find solutions to do it better the next time.

## Be sincere with yourself and others

A big part of imposter syndrome is feeling like you don't belong. But if you're clear about who you are and what you stand for, you are less likely to try to fit into a mold that wasn't designed for you in the first place. It's only after you're able to own who you authentically are that you can forge your unique path forward and become the kind of leader others want to follow. Being insincere with yourself is a trait that will lose you both supporters and respect.

Reflect on what makes you tick, what makes you comfortable or uncomfortable, and what values you stand for. For example, you might realize that you're normally reserved and subdued in large meetings but are more comfortable stating your opinions in smaller groups. Think about how you can still contribute in larger settings without feeling intimidated. Or start small: Practice being your authentic self in low-risk environments until you're more confident, and then it will come naturally to you.

## Realize you don't have to have all the answers

You'd be hard-pressed to find someone who is skilled at everything. You have strengths and weaknesses. It's useful to be aware of your weaknesses so that you can improve and grow. But you should also capitalize on your strengths. Those strengths are what got you to where you are today.

For example, if you're a people person, use that skill to increase your influence on your team. In meetings, contribute to the topics in which you have expertise. Remember that you're in the room because of your unique knowledge, just as others are in the room because of what they offer. Your goal is to work together as a group to reach your organization's missions or objectives. This can't be done by just one person. No one person has all the answers.

## Find an ally

If you're still feeling like an imposter after practicing these tips, find an ally or group of allies to be your support system. My allies have always come in the form of peer coaches: organic, mutually trusting relationships with peers I'm comfortable taking feedback from because I believe they have my best interests at heart.

Some organizations have a peer-coach program that matches individuals with one another. If your organization does not, there are other ways to form these relationships.

Ask someone whom you respect and get along with if they will peer-coach you, and hopefully they will accept. It can be a simple, "I really appreciate your insights. It would be great if I could lean on your guidance and get feedback on how you think I'm doing in this role. Would you be my peer coach? I am happy to reciprocate if that would be of benefit to you."

The benefit of having a peer coach within your company is that they see you firsthand at work every day. They observe your behaviors, witness your contributions, and can give you unbiased, independent feedback. They can point out your strengths (which will, again, do wonders for boosting your confidence), and they can advise you on areas for improvement.

. . .

A certain level of self-doubt at work can be good: It pushes us to work harder. But own your strengths so that you see what everyone else sees—that you are not an imposter. You are there because you have shown what you can do. You're an asset.

*Adapted from "Do You Ever Second Guess Yourself?" Ascend, on hbr.org, July 28, 2021.*

# 9

# Two Entrepreneurs on Facing Fear and Making Change

A conversation with Stacey Abrams and Lara Hodgson

Stacey Abrams and Lara Hodgson met in the lunch line at their Leadership Atlanta class kickoff event. They struck up a conversation, became friends, and went on to start three companies together. In their book, *Level Up: Rise Above the Hidden Forces Holding Your Business Back*, they share plenty of hard-won lessons. By describing their successes and failures, they hope to smooth the path for other entrepreneurs, especially women and women of color.

In this conversation, *Women at Work* cohost Emily Caulfield talks to Stacey and Lara to hear more about their experiences and how they've dealt with fear and self-doubt.

EMILY CAULFIELD: In the book you say, "Sometimes what's holding you back is not a glass ceiling, but rather a sticky floor. Don't let your self-doubt overcome you."

Can you talk about how the two of you dealt with this in starting your businesses?

**LARA HODGSON:** I deal with it every day. Women and underrepresented founders tend to constantly ask themselves, *Am I good enough? Am I smart enough? Am I approaching it the right way?* That's what is so valuable about our partnership, because as individuals, you're always going to wonder, *Am I missing something?* Our partnership keeps us grounded when we're worried about that. But it's also there to keep you grounded when you're going off into left field, and you need someone to say, "Bring it back in."

**STACEY ABRAMS:** One of the corollaries is that self-doubt is often driven by fear, and I believe in the legitimacy of fear. We are exhorted, especially women in business, that you're supposed to be fearless. That is the dumbest advice, because fears are real, they are salient, and they come from something.

One thing Lara and I do so effectively is confront the fear. We don't ignore it, we don't pretend it doesn't exist. Instead, we investigate the roots of it and figure out how we can befriend it, navigate it, leverage it. It's easier to do that when you have a business partner and a friend, but it's possible even if you're on your own.

Both Lara and I came to this having done other projects independent of each other, and we brought with us the fears that we had in those experiences, as well as the learnings from those fears and our willingness to share them with each other. Part of the sticky floor is that you're fighting yourself and you're fighting the legitimacy of those warnings. Fear exists because you're trying to tell yourself there's danger. So, let's make sure you're not ignoring the warning signs, but are investigating and preparing for the danger.

**EMILY:** You both brought up an interesting point about being women in business. Do you feel like being women helped or hindered you as you launched your businesses?

**STACEY:** Yes.

**EMILY:** Both?

**STACEY:** I mean, there are doors that get cracked open just so they can see that you're out there. It doesn't necessarily mean they're going to invite you in. A lot of women experience this with programs that are geared toward women. And as a woman of color myself, there's never the ability to leave behind the dimension of race when gender is also part of the conversation.

There have been moments where we've had to confront both pieces—there are expectations that come along with gender, some that come with race, some that come together—and the challenge is often in trying to understand which you're facing. But the opportunity is in understanding how you can leverage the diversity and the distinction of who you are to differentiate yourself.

So as women in business, we often see problems in a different way. We are used to having to navigate and circumnavigate challenges. The same thing is true for people of color. Part of what has helped our business relationship is that we bring our different perspectives from gender and these other dimensions into how we problem solve. Because we aren't going to have access to the traditional resources, and we're not going to have the standard opportunities that others may take for granted. Our responsibility is to figure out how we get where we need to be, not *despite* who we are, but recognizing that what people see isn't going to change even if we close our eyes really tight and hope they don't notice. You decide how you're going to leverage it, and you prepare for when it is used against you.

LARA: I've always believed that your greatest strength is also your greatest weakness, and there are times when it's your choice how to use it—meaning the mindset that you approach it with could determine whether that becomes your strength or your weakness.

For example, I am often on panels in the fintech space where I am the only female. And when I'm in that situation, I say to myself, "I'm the only woman on this panel. That is my superpower." I'm not going to try to blend in;

in fact, it's quite the opposite. I'm probably going to wear a very bright statement necklace, and I am going to say something bold that makes the audience uncomfortable. I'm going to do that because you are going to remember me.

**STACEY:** Part of it is also whether what you're addressing is structural and institutional, or situational. One of the reasons we wrote the book, which is related to one way we've both operated in business and one reason we both found our way into politics and organizations, is we recognize that sometimes the short-term solution is situational but the long-term solution is institutional. For a lot of small business owners, and for a lot of women, we believe that it's a bifurcated choice. We have to pick one or the other, or we are so overwhelmed by the systemic challenge that we abandon all hope and focus on the situational.

What we want to encourage is an understanding that the institutional side is just people—really, really powerful people supported by less powerful people, supported by people who don't think they can make things change.

I like to say we're instigators—we insert ourselves into the institutions. Part of the opportunity when you face those challenges is to insert yourself into the organizations that perpetuate them, and you don't go in saying, "I'm going to destroy you from the inside." You don't come in as the conqueror. You come in as the inquisitor: You get yourself inside, start to work, and create change from inside.

One of our most effective approaches is that we work from the inside out and from the outside in. We both come from different vantage points, but we carry the same internal messaging. We get points of entry that are completely divergent from each other, and then people are shocked when they find out that we've met in the middle and have put our efforts toward changing the way things work. We sometimes let the size and scale of the challenge overwhelm us, and we become myopically focused on the situational to the exclusion of the systemic. But if we don't fix or address the systemic, the system just gets more hardened. We have to understand our power to be solution makers for the situational and the institutional as well.

*Adapted from "Stacey Abrams and Lara Hodgson on Starting and Scaling a Small Business,"* Women at Work *podcast, bonus episode, February 21, 2022.*

SECTION FOUR

# Establish Your Authority

# 10

# Build a Strong Reputation for Yourself

by Dorie Clark

We all know that developing a personal brand is valuable, since a strong reputation can put you on the radar for exciting career opportunities. When your true talents are understood, you're far more likely to be tapped for relevant and interesting assignments—and it helps you stand out in a field of competitors. Research by economist and author Sylvia Ann Hewlett shows that cultivating your personal brand is one of the best ways to attract a sponsor—and professionals with sponsors are 23% more likely than their peers to be promoted.[1] Your brand is also a powerful hedge against professional misfortune: If there are layoffs or cutbacks at your company, being recognized in your field makes it far more likely that you'll be snapped up quickly by another firm.

But personal branding has some unique challenges for female professionals. Research has repeatedly shown that women are subject to a phenomenon known as the "likability conundrum." Gender norms presume that women should be agreeable, warm, and nurturing, and when they violate these norms—such as when they step up to make a tough decision, share a strong opinion, or promote themselves—they're often penalized for that behavior in a way that men wouldn't be. We can all think of examples of women who have been publicly criticized for being "too aggressive" or labeled an "ice queen" or the "b-word."

How can women navigate this conundrum and develop a robust personal brand? Here are three strategies that can help ensure your talents are recognized.

## Network Both Inside and Outside Your Organization

Too many professionals overindex on "bonding capital," to use a term popularized by Harvard sociologist Robert Putnam, and underinvest in "bridging capital." In other words, they have too many connections who are like them (working in the same company or the same industry) and not nearly enough who are dissimilar.

When only a select group knows about your talents and abilities, you put yourself in jeopardy. There are fewer people who can speak to your contributions or provide support, whether that's help in securing additional resources for an important project or in moving up to a new role. And if your department is reorganized or your company has layoffs, the people who understand your talents won't be in a position to help.

Instead, consciously cultivate a broad network, so if your situation changes or you need backup, you have options. For instance, you could make a point of building professional connections with people you meet through hobbies, relationships of proximity (say, neighbors or parents at your kids' school), or friends of friends.

## Control Your Narrative

We often assume that if we work hard people will notice it over time, or that if we've made a transition it will intuitively make sense to others. Because people are so overstretched these days, that's unfortunately almost never true. They're simply not paying close enough attention to our professional trajectory to formulate a coherent narrative of us. Worse, they may make inaccurate assumptions—such as that your skills must be wildly out of date since you took time off after having a child, or that you shifted to functional roles because you "couldn't hack it"—which could cause you to miss out on growth opportunities.

Help others understand your journey by developing a clear and concise elevator pitch that explains how your previous experiences connect with, and add value to, what you're doing now. Make that connection explicit, rather than hoping others will figure it out on their own.

To start, chart it out on paper. On one side, write down your past positions or experiences. On the other side, write down the job you currently hold. Then find the connective tissue that links them.

For instance, your past might be "HR director" and your present might be "regional sales leader." An outsider may have no idea what connects these two positions and assume your career path is somewhat random. But you know that your experience in HR taught you about how to listen empathetically, understand what motivates people, and develop win-win solutions—which are perfect ingredients for sales success. When you're able to share this with others, they'll almost always get it and recognize the unique skills you bring to your position and the organization.

A crisp elevator pitch isn't useful just for times when you're job hunting. There are often opportunities to shape the way you're perceived by others, but most people miss them. For instance, new acquaintances will ask how long you've been at your job or how you came to your current field. Having a pithy answer means you can turn their question into an opportunity to subtly highlight your skills: "I started out in HR and worked my way up to director. But I became fascinated by the sales process, and realized the listening skills and ability to connect with people that I'd developed in HR would enable me to add real value to the company, so I transitioned last year and am now the head of northeast sales." You haven't just laid out your job titles; you've provided context that conveys a strong personal brand.

Similarly, during performance reviews, you can make a point of reminding your boss about how you're leveraging key strengths you've developed over time. For instance, you could connect this year's increase in client upsells to your work developing your team's listening skills so that they're more attuned to client needs.

## Share Your Ideas Publicly

If you keep a low profile and let your work speak for itself, you may indeed develop a good reputation among the people you work closely with. But that's a relatively limited number of people. Individuals in other departments or leaders many levels above you may not be aware of your contributions, and any staffing changes might disrupt the hard-fought-for reputational capital you've built. A new boss or colleagues, lacking personal experience with you, may have no idea whether you're any good.

Many women may feel uncomfortable talking about their accomplishments and promoting themselves directly, but there are other ways to show your areas of expertise when building a brand. Content creation is a good way to share your ideas and build a positive reputation at scale. The precise mechanics will differ based on company policies (for example, in certain regulated industries your ability to use social media may be limited), but in almost any organization there are ways to demonstrate your knowledge and help others.

For instance, you could volunteer to host a lunch-and-learn about a topic you've been researching, start writing for the company newsletter, or offer advice or respond to queries on the corporate intranet. Many professionals ignore these opportunities, assuming they're distractions that take them away from their "real work" or scoffing that no one really pays attention to them. Even if these opportunities are not popular among your colleagues, higher-ups are almost always paying attention, since they view these channels as important vehicles for transferring knowledge and sharing best practices. One college friend of mine, while working as a sales clerk at a large retailer, got into a private message exchange with the company CEO—eventually winning a trip to headquarters as the result of one of her posts on the corporate intranet.

Content creation may also open up completely unexpected opportunities, including new jobs. Miranda Aisling, whom I profile in my book *Stand Out*, self-published a book about creativity that she gave to a friend who worked at an arts organization. He liked it and passed it along to his supervisor; when Aisling later applied for a job at the organization, she was a shoo-in because the book had already established her credibility in the field.

Personal branding is fraught for many professionals—no one wants to look like a craven self-promoter. And with the likability conundrum, building meaningful connections and a strong reputation at work is even more complicated for women.

But if we don't control our own narratives and show the world what we can contribute, odds are that very few people will actually notice. By following these strategies, you dramatically increase the odds that your true talents will be known, recognized, and appreciated.

*Adapted from "How Women Can Develop—and Promote—Their Personal Brand," on hbr.org, March 2, 2018 (product #H046PA).*

# 11

# Get Comfortable "Playing Politics" at Work

by Lisa Zigarmi, Julie Diamond, and Lesli Mones

Office politics. It's a term many people cringe at. Broadly defined, playing politics is the ability to successfully navigate the unwritten rules of how things get done at work and through whom. That includes understanding the motivations of others and using this knowledge to influence people in ways that enhance one's personal interests and organizational objectives.

In our experience as psychologists and coaches, we have found that many women have an adverse, almost allergic reaction to office politics. Numerous studies confirm this: Women tend to see it as something "dirty" or dishonest and as a stressful aspect of work that reduces their job satisfaction.[1]

Yet humans are relational beings by nature, and political skill matters—it is a necessary part of organizational life. Studies affirm that being able to successfully use political skills is critical to career advancement.[2]

We recognize that engaging in office politics can be stressful. It often forces people to stretch beyond their natural preferences and patterns. We aim to offer ways to participate in politics that reduce discomfort and maximize career advancement.

There are five commonly held beliefs underlying women's aversion to being political at work:

1. **My work should speak for itself.** Playing politics contradicts many people's belief in meritocracy. The notion that one has to do more than excel at work is anathema to many men and women alike. However, for women and other marginalized groups who have to work twice as hard to counter biases related to their gender and race, playing politics can be an even greater insult and burden.

2. **Building connections is an extracurricular activity.** Cultivating political relationships often feels extraneous and distracting from the work, like just another item on a to-do list. And for women, who spend an average of 37% more time than men on housework and chores in addition to their full-time jobs, the idea that they have to find more

space and time for these additional activities feels unreasonable.[3]

3. **It's inauthentic.** Politics is often seen as posturing, making alliances with those who have clout or supporting initiatives that are popular simply for the sake of staying close to the power source. To many, this can feel inauthentic and, at times, duplicitous.

4. **I don't like playing hardball.** Office politics often plays out as a zero-sum game, involving gossip, backstabbing, sabotaging, and even intimidation. Women, and a fair number of men, have an aversion to these tactics and prefer power that is based on influence, relationships, and win-win approaches.

5. **The penalties are too great.** Women are penalized for displaying political skill. A number of studies show that women are judged more harshly for being assertive or competitive, two common characteristics of office politics. Consequently, they see negative reactions and repercussions for it.

Do you hold any of these beliefs? If so, it's understandable. There's validity to them. And yet, if you don't challenge them, you may be limiting your potential.

In our work, we have found that making five shifts in mindset is an effective way to counter these beliefs and embrace political skills.

## From "My work should speak for itself" to "It's my responsibility to show people how my work connects to theirs"

No one is an island. When people, male or female, believe their work should speak for itself, they fail to recognize the interdependence of organizational life. Believing your work should speak for itself is a narrow, functional view of a job, one that assumes others can fully appreciate and comprehend the part you play in the larger organizational puzzle.

We typically see this belief in two groups. The first is very technical leaders—those with a highly valued, specialized area of expertise. It's easy for these individuals to see how the organization depends on what they provide, but it's less obvious to them how their work depends on others.

We also have heard this response from those who are more comfortable with a hierarchical style of leadership and who have a more deferential relationship with management. They question the necessity of advocating for themselves, thinking that seeing and evaluating their performance is their manager's task.

When we work with people on making a shift away from this mindset, we focus on transitioning from a functional or expert mindset to an enterprise one, enabling them to connect their area of expertise to the larger business needs. In other words, they need to think in terms of what's best for the whole organization, not just their small part of it.

One of us coached a senior executive who rose rapidly through the ranks from director to vice president in a technical, male-dominated field. She navigated the politics in her rise to the top by learning how to connect her work to others'. Before every conversation, every meeting, and every presentation, she would set aside five minutes to anticipate the possible blowback or resistance she could incur. She took a careful inventory of her audience, considering who they were, what their needs were, and what priorities they had. She would then think about ways to connect her contributions to their needs, positioning herself as a necessary and intrinsic part of everyone else's success. By carefully tying her work to others' and to the organization's goals, she tied her success to the success of others, thereby ensuring that they saw the value in what she had to offer.

## From "Building connections is an extracurricular activity" to "Building connections is a force multiplier"

Work gets done with and through people. And the higher up you go, the more this is true. In the interdependent world of work, where you need others to help you accomplish your goals, continuously nurturing relationships and learning from others is key to your success.

For example, attending a women's conference can double a woman's likelihood of receiving a promotion within a year, triple her likelihood of getting a 10%+ pay increase within a year, and immediately increase her sense of optimism by up to 78%.[4] Something powerful happens when people engage with others: They are more inspired. They learn new strategies for career advancement. They are exposed to new ideas. They build confidence in asking for what they need. And maybe they even find a way to share their wisdom with others.

When we work with leaders on making a mindset shift about the power of building connections, we help them see the benefits, not just the burden, of doing so. We host six-month leadership development programs within organizations where participants have the opportunity to meet, repeatedly, as cohorts. Women who are seeking new opportunities, are stuck in their career trajectory, or are struggling with leadership tensions find it useful to hear from others in similar positions, learn new approaches for promoting themselves, and see alternatives for managing their challenges.

In the final session, participants give a five-minute presentation on a topic that has big career implications after rehearsing and revising their presentations in small groups. These dress rehearsals give people the opportunity to hone their stories, more clearly articulate their facts, and bolster their stage presence for maximum effectiveness. Countless participants credit the feedback from their new network with helping them adjust and sharpen their presentations to the point that they ultimately land funding, drive new strategy, and galvanize followers. In several instances, the women have also helped each other find new roles, transition into different departments, and gain access to new and influential networks. In other words, the relationships built in the program and the perspectives gathered from those relationships help our participants amplify their impact.

## From "It's inauthentic" to "I'm being paid to have a point of view and share it"

The research on authenticity shows that it requires two things: conscious awareness (knowing who you are, what your motives are, and what you're bringing to the current situation) and expression (consciously aligning your behavior with your awareness).[5] This means acting in accordance with your true feelings, thoughts, and highest intentions in a way that serves the context. Authenticity requires discernment, courage, and self-determination. It's not reacting to what's happening around you; it's relating to the players and situation from a grounded sense of who you are.

You're more negatively affected by office politics if you don't know what you stand for or don't have the courage to advocate for it. To be political—and authentic—you must know what your values and intentions are so that you can move projects and teams forward in a way that aligns with your and the organization's goals.

In some ways, it's easier for people to be against politics than to get clear on what they stand for and champion it. When we work with people on making a shift in this mindset, we help them discern their purpose and values so that they can make choices in alignment with them.

One of us coached a woman who was discouraged by the leadership behavior of the senior leaders in her business unit. As a result, rather than seeking promotion to the next level, she was considering quitting. Through coaching, she realized that although her decision was a reaction to her colleagues' behavior, she hadn't defined the leadership behavior she valued. By clarifying her own leadership point of view, she felt inspired to model new behaviors and open up conversations inside her business unit about the role leaders play in creating the culture. This changed her attitude toward her job, and she felt more inspired and motivated to stay in the role and even apply for a promotion. Rather than reacting to what she disliked, she made a conscious decision to be a role model for the leadership behavior she wanted to see present in her organization.

## From "I'm not someone who plays hardball" to "My leadership tactic needs to match the situation"

Political behavior can be a turnoff, especially when it involves hard power tactics: coercion, intimidation, and sabotage. For many people, men and women alike, this is what "being political" means, as opposed to using softer power tactics of persuading, building alliances, and offering assistance.

Yet power, whether hard or soft, is neither good nor bad. What makes the use of power good or bad is the motivation behind its use and the impact it has on others. While it's easy to see the negative applications of hard power, soft power can also be misused, or used to villainous ends. Consider how Bernie Madoff, Jeffrey Skilling, and Jim Jones employed persuasion, charisma, and relationship building.

When we work with leaders on making a shift away from this mindset, we help them understand that their application of hard or soft power tactics should be situational, not a matter of preference or style. Some situations call for hard power and some for soft power. Specifically, hard power tactics may be needed to hold people accountable, make tough and unpopular decisions, set boundaries, or enact consequences to inappropriate workplace behavior.

One of us coached a leader who had a decided preference for soft power tactics. She was in a creative industry in which her collaborative style worked well at first. But a few months after she started leading a new team, individuals began to complain about burnout. Shortly thereafter, a few senior team members quit due to conflict. This led her to look at the group's dynamics and how her leadership was a factor.

Through discussions with each team member, she realized that her collaborative approach had resulted in meetings being dominated and derailed by a few vocal members. Agendas were often hijacked by tangential discussions and meetings often ended without clarity and direction, forcing people to spend hours in discussion to recap and rehash the outcomes.

Our client learned to incorporate hard power tactics to match the team dynamic. She began to intervene, set boundaries, create rules for conversation, and hold people accountable if they failed to follow the meeting guidelines. It was a revelation to her to realize that collaborative leadership has its limits and that harder power tactics can also have a place.

## From "The penalties are too great" to "I prioritize my growth"

Women are penalized for being ambitious and displaying political skill. The research is clear: Negative stereotypes have negative consequences for one's career.[6] It's true that women and minorities pay a steep price for displaying ambition.

Yet, for many, the alternative may be worse. While the blowback to displaying ambition is tough, so too is the personal and psychological toll of not striving to fulfill your potential and not stretching to reach your goals. For many women and minorities, waiting for the world to change before they can assert themselves is a steeper price to pay than the backlash of being ambitious.

The mindset here is one of prioritizing growth. But this shouldn't be done naively. It's important to be prepared and to consider the consequences you may face. You may need to gather resources and allies and to ensure you have support in your personal and professional life before undertaking any action. Above all, it's important to have a plan B, or even a plan C, in place. Consider, realistically, the penalties you may face. Do you have alternatives in mind if things don't work out as planned? Are you prepared to switch business units or even companies if necessary?

A growth mindset (the belief that talents can be developed through hard work, good strategies, and input from others) is protective against negative stereotypes. For example, one study found that when Black university students were taught to have a growth mindset, they were less likely to internalize the negative stereotypes directed at them, and thus had better outcomes in their studies.[7] On the other hand, students with a fixed mindset, seeing themselves as unable to change, were more prone to suffer the effects of the negative stereotyping.

One of us coached a woman who described her manager as someone who stifled her ambition, denied her access to senior leaders, and routinely took credit for her work. She felt pushed out by her manager, with no option but to leave the firm. Through coaching she realized that she had, in fact, mastered her role: There wasn't room to learn new skills, create more impact, or meet new stakeholders. Her lack of opportunity had as much to do with her role's limited scope as with her disparaging manager.

By recognizing her need for growth, she decided to seek a new role with more scope and impact potential outside her firm. Rather than feeling "chased out," she realized her old position was more limiting than her leader. This mindset shift made her the hero of the story instead of the victim.

The harsh reality is that women and racial minorities face discrimination, negative stereotypes, and hostility. But there are choices to be made, choices that provide more, or less, flexibility and resilience. Preparing yourself, gathering allies and resources, having a plan B in place, and developing a growth mindset that frames the challenge as an opportunity to learn and grow can be powerful protection against the backlash you may face.

. . .

Office politics impacts your work experience and projects whether you participate in it or not. We suggest that it's better to be a player than a pawn. The women we coach want to be leading at the highest levels, yet many have not examined their limiting beliefs about using political skills to advance their careers. The mindset you bring to any situation, especially one that can be experienced as negative and aversive, is critical to your success.

Office politics matters because, as relational beings, getting ahead is as much about people and relationships as it is about skills and experience. Your ability to participate in politics—and to employ your political skills—is not just critical to career advancement but also important for your well-being at work.

*Adapted from "How Women Can Get Comfortable 'Playing Politics' at Work," on hbr.org, January 19, 2022 (product #H06T5D).*

# 12

# What to Do When People Doubt Your Expertise

A conversation with Raven Hoffman and Vanessa Bohns

Raven Hoffman, like a lot of us, is trying to figure out how to better persuade others. She works in the construction industry as a senior estimator at a tile and stone contractor.

Construction is one of the most male-dominated industries in the world. Raven has been in it for 20 years, thriving and with no plans to leave. But she's been struggling with a new important part of her job: selling people she hasn't met before on doing business with her and her company. Conversations and meetings she's initiated haven't consistently forged the sorts of trusting relationships that lead to contracts. But Raven is determined to become more persuasive with prospective and existing clients, as well as with longtime colleagues.

In this conversation, *Women at Work* cohost Amy Gallo speaks to Raven alongside Vanessa Bohns, a social psychologist, a professor at Cornell University, and the author of *You Have More Influence Than You Think*, to discuss advice for preempting people from doubting your expertise and establishing relationships that will extend your influence inside and outside your company.

AMY GALLO: Raven, where do you feel like you have influence, and where do you think you lack it in your work?

RAVEN HOFFMAN: I am fortunate. In the company I work for, the current ownership came on when their grandmother was running the company; they believe in hiring strong women. They believe in letting us do what we do best, and they listen within the company. Often it's externally that my knowledge seems to be under question.

AMY: Is that with customers, with subcontractors?

RAVEN: Customers. Often I will call with an issue on a project to say, "I foresee this as an upcoming problem," and the response I get is, "Hey, is your boss there? Can I talk to him about it?" Usually I transfer them over to him, and he laughs at them and says, "You need to talk to Raven. She knows what's going on more than I do" and sends them back. But I think they've already disengaged from me as an authority who knows what she's talking about.

**AMY:** Vanessa, in your research, you explore people's perception of their influence and how that compares with reality. What did you hear in Raven's answer that speaks to the common perceptions or misperceptions that women tend to have about their power to be persuasive?

**VANESSA BOHNS:** I definitely hear some elements of the way we use stereotypes to understand people we don't know well. If we go into an interaction with someone, and we don't know how to behave with this person or what we think of this person, stereotypes guide us in a way of thinking about them and how the interaction is going to go.

Unfortunately, in many places in the world, seeing a woman brings to mind the stereotype that they don't have as much expertise, particularly if it's in a field that tends to be male-dominated. On the other hand, the people who really do know you—who know that you have this expertise or you have these established relationships—they don't need to rely on a stereotype, right? They actually know you.

This is a classic way of coding people we don't know. One of the things that women tend to get dinged on, in terms of the stereotypes, is this idea that we aren't authorities on something, particularly if it's in a male-dominated field.

**AMY:** Like construction?

**VANESSA:** Exactly. We know from the literature on influence that we listen to people who we think are authorities. If someone who we think knows what they're talking about tells us that we should do something, not surprisingly, we assume that we should do it, rather than thinking, *Oh, this person doesn't know what they're talking about.* But women often face a sort of double whammy. There's this coding of, *OK, this person is not as much of an authority as their male counterpart*, but also women often struggle to profess their authority.

I was part of a project where we learned how to write op-eds to get more female and underrepresented minorities into public discourse. One of the activities they had us do was to establish our authority: *Why am I the one to write this op-ed?* We would go around the room and say, "Here's who I am. I went to this school. I have this background . . ." And women with these extraordinary backgrounds would play them down. Women who had done amazing things were like, "Yeah, I know how to do this little thing" when in fact they had studied it for 10 years and were masters at it.

So, one thing women can do to make up for that authority gap is profess our authority. For example, you can say, "Hi, I'm so-and-so. Here's my long list of expertise, and this is why I'm talking to you." What that really says is, "OK, you may have had a stereotype about me. We're going to get rid of that right here and now, and I'm going to tell you exactly why I have the authority to be talking to you."

But women tend to hesitate to do that. And in this case, the fact that your boss is just saying "You should talk to Raven" without giving you that buildup—it's putting you at a disadvantage.

**AMY:** Raven, how do you introduce yourself when you're working with new clients? Have you tried what Vanessa's describing?

**RAVEN:** I have not, and I'm really intrigued about what that would end up looking like in a conversation—without coming across as arrogant by saying, "Hey, I know you're new. Let me pile on you how many years I've been doing this and how much I know." How would you work that into the conversation without coming across as arrogant?

**VANESSA:** That's exactly why the women in my group hesitated to talk about all their accolades. They were worried they were going to come across as bragging and arrogant.

Really, when we're judged by other people, we tend to be judged on two main things: warmth and competence. Women tend to be judged even more on warmth. So, if we overplay our competence, people think we're cold, and that's where we come across as arrogant.

Unfortunately, the best way to counteract that is to couple your expressions of competence with something warm. It could be something like, "I am so excited to work with you because I have worked with so many other clients," or something similar that sounds good. "I have been working in this field for 15 or 20 years because I just love it, and I can't wait to work with you." Something that says, "Look at all this experience I have," but in this warm, friendly, cooperative sort of way.

**AMY:** How does that land with you, Raven?

**RAVEN:** I like that. I can do that.

**AMY:** I can even imagine saying, "I've been assigned to this project because I've done 4,000 just like it. I'm really excited to collaborate with you to get your project done on time and under budget," or whatever metrics matter to your clients.

**VANESSA:** That would be great. As you said, you want to know the metrics that matter to them—what would establish to them that you're an expert. You put that out there and add something that says, "I'm telling you this so that we can have a great relationship and so I can be helpful." That gets it across for sure.

**AMY:** One of the pieces of advice I've heard given is, if you want to persuade someone, you need to demonstrate that you yourself are persuadable. Is that advice that you agree with, Vanessa? And if so, how do you show that you're willing to change your mind?

**VANESSA:** Yeah, that's a helpful tactic, because one of the fundamental aspects of human behavior is reciprocity. So, I give a little, you give a little. Once I give, you feel this kind of urge or need to give a little back. No one wants to be the jerk who's like, *You just made this major concession and now I'm going to stand my ground.*

It also makes the other person feel listened to. If you can give something, it shows that you're not just in it for yourself. That makes it a more cooperative integrative discussion, which we tend to forget when we're trying to persuade someone. We think we're on two sides, and I'm pushing while you're pulling. But when you give a little, it says, "I see your side, I am willing to consider this integratively. I'm willing to give up a little bit myself. Now, what are you willing to do?" It becomes a more cooperative discussion.

**RAVEN:** One of our company owners says that, quite often with customers, I go from the salesperson Raven to their friend Raven by the end of the project. Well, if I'm their friend, they're going to be more likely to refer me. It's getting to that point where they realize I do actually care. You can't fake wanting someone to have a successful project, and they feel that.

**VANESSA:** So many people are uncomfortable with things like negotiation and sales, and part of that is because the discomfort makes us think of one-shot interactions—*I'm just going to get in there and do it. I'm* *going to make the sale. I'm going to convince someone. I'm going to get it done.* In fact, the best kinds of sales and negotiations are long-term relationships. As soon as you start thinking of it in those terms—the next time I have to sell to this person, the next time we negotiate—it changes the way you approach it for the better.

**AMY:** Let's say you have tried to persuade your boss or your team to do something and it hasn't gone well. You've failed, but you still believe it's a cause worth pursuing or pushing. What should you do before you try again?

**VANESSA:** This is a case where I would try to generate as much curiosity as possible, because if I think it's an important enough issue that I'm willing to go back and push for it, but other people don't seem to see my side, I'd be really curious: What's keeping people from doing this? How are they seeing things so differently from me?

I would get into question-asking mode. I would take a step out of my initial, *I'm going to change things, I'm going to persuade* mode and get into a mode of, *I'm going to understand, I'm going to ask questions.* That's where you learn what the actual barriers are to getting them to see your side, and you might learn that there is an advantage. They're getting something out of doing this their way that you didn't see, and maybe you can find a way for them to still get that thing and for you to get what you need as well. A lot of what you do next is dependent on the answers you get from those follow-up interviews after you've failed to persuade.

**AMY:** Raven, what are you taking away from this conversation? What do you feel like you might do differently?

**RAVEN:** I'm definitely going to work on building allies in conversations and meetings with new people. I'm going to keep pursuing the goal of becoming that authority—and doing it gently, as opposed to with a sledgehammer—so that I can build those relationships, because everything in life is about those continued relationships. If I do something incorrectly in the beginning, it can cause damage moving forward, and I want to use the correct persuasion tactics. I've gotten a lot of wonderful tools to be able to do that.

*Adapted from "The Essentials: Persuading People,"* Women at Work *podcast, bonus episode, April 11, 2022.*

# 13

# Feeling Underappreciated or Undervalued at Work?

by Rebecca Knight

It's no fun to toil away at a job where your efforts go unnoticed. How can you highlight your achievements at work without bragging? Who should you talk to about feeling underappreciated? And if the situation doesn't change, how long should you stay?

"There's nothing worse than feeling unseen and unheard in the workplace," says Annie McKee, author of *How to Be Happy at Work*. "We all have a human need to be appreciated for our efforts, so when your colleagues don't notice [your contributions], it makes you feel as though you don't belong." You might also start to worry—justifiably—about your potential professional advancement. "Self-doubt starts to creep in, and you think, 'If no one notices what I'm doing, how am I going to get ahead?'"

But you are not powerless to change the situation, says Karen Dillon, author of the *HBR Guide to Office Politics*. "There are many ways to make sure people understand and see what you do." The key, she says, is to find "diplomatic ways to toot your own horn." Here are some ideas.

## Assess the Situation

Before you take any action, think about the amount of appreciation and feedback you expect from your organization. "People are very busy. The feedback might not be as much as you want," but it might be reasonable within the context of your organization, says Dillon. "You are dealing with human beings. . . . Even with good intentions, your colleagues and manager might overlook what you do and take you for granted."

When you're feeling unappreciated, Dillon recommends running a "personal litmus test" on your recent accomplishments. Ask yourself, "Was my work extraordinary? Was it over and above what my peers typically do?" And importantly, "If I had to ask for credit for it, would I sound like a jerk?" If you're unsure, she suggests seeking a second opinion from a "slightly senior colleague" or a peer you "deeply respect."

## Talk to Your Boss

When your efforts are going unsung, engage your boss in a conversation, says McKee. Granted, this will be easier with some managers than others. "The average boss doesn't pay attention to human needs," says McKee. If yours falls into that category, keep in mind that "you're not going to change that person, but you can signal that you'd like more dialogue on your performance," she says. "And if your boss is average to good, they might heed the call." Of course, you must be subtle. "Don't go in saying, 'I want more appreciation.'" Instead, McKee recommends saying something along the lines of, "I'd like to talk about the past three months and get a sense of where my strengths lie and where I could learn." Come prepared with specific examples, advises Dillon. She suggests drawing up a list of your recent achievements to jog your manager's memory of your good work. "Most managers are happy to have that list," she says.

## Increase Your Team's Visibility

If you manage a team, you also need to look for ways to explain to others what the group does and why it's valuable, says Dillon. "In our hectic daily lives, your boss and colleagues might not be aware of" the ins and outs of your job. She advises asking your own manager for a sliver of time to "talk about what your team does, what its goals are, and ways you're striving to do better."

McKee also suggests more subtle ways to draw attention to the group's day-to-day efforts. For example, don't let presentations or reports go out without being clear about who created them. "Make sure everyone's name goes on the work product," she says. You want people beyond your manager to see what your team is delivering. Spread credit—don't hoard it—when it's due. But don't be afraid to tout your own leadership. "Sometimes, in your efforts to be inclusive and not sound self-aggrandizing, you miss an opportunity," Dillon explains. Women tend to do this more than men, she notes. It's OK to "use the word 'I,' as in 'I accomplished X and Y, and I am grateful for the support that I had.'"

## Recognize Others' Contributions

One surefire way to get your work noticed is, "paradoxically," to "praise and appreciate others," says McKee. "By being the person who notices a job well done, you can be the agent of change" in your organization's culture. Most often the "response from the other person will be to return the favor," she adds. If your boss is not one to dispense positive feedback, talk to your team about "what you can do to shore each other up" and generate optimism among the ranks. "Because of the pace of our organizations, what we produce becomes passé or invisible fast," notes McKee. She recommends creating norms in your team such that when a colleague makes an important contribution or finishes a piece of work, "everyone stops for a nanosecond and says, 'Yay.'" But Dillon cautions against getting carried away. "Sending extensive thank-yous can diminish the message," she says. "Use your judgment. Ask, 'Who really deserves acknowledgement for going the extra mile?'"

## Validate Yourself

While being appreciated and valued for your work is a wonderful thing, you can't expect all your "motivation to come from honors, accolades, and public gratitude," says Dillon. Intrinsic motivators are much more powerful. "You need to strive to find meaning in the work itself." McKee concurs. "Ultimately, over the course of your working life, you want to move away from the need for external validation," she says. "Real fulfillment comes from within."

Make an effort to pat yourself on the back regularly. "Try to carve out time at the end of each week to reflect on what went well and what didn't go as well," suggests McKee. This is a useful exercise for remembering both what you're good at and why you do what you do. "Be careful not to sink into deficiency mode, where you [dwell on] everything you did wrong," she adds. "Catalog the wins."

## Consider Moving On

If you continue to feel undervalued and unappreciated by your company, it might be a sign that it's not the right place for you. "We all stay in jobs that aren't perfect for a lot of reasons," says McKee. Maybe you need the experience, or perhaps you can't move because you need to be in a certain geographic region for your spouse or partner. But if you've tried to make the job more validating and fulfilling, and nothing has worked, it might be time to look for a new one.

*Adapted from "What to Do When You Don't Feel Valued at Work," on hbr.org, December 26, 2017 (product #H0433N).*

SECTION FIVE

# Fight Back Against Bias and Microaggressions

14

# How to React to Incidents of Bias at Work

by Judith Honesty, David Maxfield, and Joseph Grenny

Bias at work can be overt and insidious. It can be shocking and enraging. But the subtle "Wait, what just happened?" moments are far more frequent. Take these examples: A client assumes you are in a subordinate role because of your age. A prospective customer only makes eye contact with your white colleague. A coworker calls you "angry" while your equally assertive male counterpart gets labeled "strong."

Moments like these leave you questioning others' intentions and your own perceptions. Your inner dialogue can sound a bit like, *I'm upset. But should I be? Do I have a right to be?* At best, this shadowy bias is exhausting. At worst, it is soul-destroying.

Bias's sometimes slippery nature also makes it difficult to eradicate in the workplace. Leaders implement policies that prohibit discrimination against protected classes, but rules can't prevent unconscious, unintentional bias. How do you legislate status assumptions, eye contact, and silent perceptions?

Clearly, organizational cultures need to change. But in the meantime, what's an individual to do who suffers daily from subtle inequities? While it's unfair to place additional burdens on victims of bias, injustice is amplified if they aren't provided with coping tools for the interim.

## Understanding Bias

In our research, we asked people who felt they had experienced bias at work to describe the incident in detail. Within two weeks we had 498 rich, passionate, and heartbreaking stories. Most described blatant actions of bias. For example:

> *I was dining with my coworkers when two gay men walked by. Several coworkers jeered and displayed disgust. As I am gay, it was very disheartening that these employees who are trained in diversity and acceptance acted both unprofessionally and impolitely. A coworker who knows I am gay told them they should know their audience, but it went right over their heads and they returned to the conversation unashamed and unaware.*

Other stories illustrated momentary lapses, where the offender tried to recover but it was usually too late. For example:

> *I'm the only woman in a team of 10 men. When I was pregnant, I told my manager at 11 weeks. He was exasperated. "That's the last time I ever hire a woman," he said. I was gobsmacked. On Monday he apologized for his comment. "I was only joking," he said. I accepted his apology, but knew he wasn't really joking. I wish I had stood up for myself.*

Paradoxically, the rarest examples are the ones that happen most often: patterns of unintentional, unconscious bias. Their scarcity in our collection is probably because they involve subtle patterns that are tough to recognize, describe, and address.

> *I am the only woman on a team of software engineers. The lead engineers, who have a lot of influence over who gets picked for the "cool," new, and groundbreaking projects, typically overlook me. I feel it's because I'd be a buzzkill in the male-locker-room atmosphere.*

The problem isn't just that people experience bias. It's that their experiences are often undiscussable. Victims don't want to call others bigots or be accused of "playing the diversity card"—actions that can be career limiting. Instead, they keep their concerns to themselves.

We asked our research participants to rate how permanent, pervasive, and controllable these incidents of bias are at work. These are the three dimensions that psychologist Martin Seligman uses to assess helplessness and hopelessness—and even depression. The results were disheartening but hardly surprising:

- **Permanent.** Forty-nine percent of victims said the bias is an enduring part of their workplace and happens regularly and routinely.
- **Pervasive.** Sixty-six percent said it impacts all aspects of their engagement, morale, motivation, commitment, and desire to advance in the organization.
- **Uncontrollable.** Sixty percent said they did not feel they could master incidents of bias in the moment or prevent them from recurring in the future.

More than a quarter of the participants (27%) described their experience with bias as the worst combination of all three: permanent, pervasive, and uncontrollable.

## Responding, Not Reacting

Victims of bias need skills to replace ulcers, invective, and silent judgment with open, honest, and respectful dialogue. While companies need to address the systemic issues within the culture itself (see the sidebar, "Strategies for Organizations"), individuals should know how to influence their workplace without alienating those they need support from. Below are skills we've seen people use successfully to address the subtleties of unconscious bias:

## Use "C.P.R."

You can choose to address issues at three levels:

- **Content:** a one-time incident
- **Pattern:** a series of incidents
- **Relationship:** the impact of a pattern on your ability to work productively with others

When an issue is overt and egregious—someone makes an intolerant comment, say—a content conversation works fine. However, with subtleties you must gather more data until you can describe a pattern. For example, if the boss repeatedly reaches out to your direct reports and not to you, be sure you can cite a few instances and draw attention to the pattern, or else your manager is likely to try to explain away the single instance you're describing. Finally, consider addressing a relationship issue by helping others understand the cumulative effect of their behaviors on trust, cooperation, self-esteem, and so on.

## Strategies for Organizations

Most organizations already have disciplinary procedures for egregious intentional bias, but many are missing strategies that can eliminate unintended, unconscious bias and those "What just happened here?" moments before they occur. The following approaches can influence cultural norms and practices to dramatically reduce unconscious bias.

**Set challenging goals and track results.** Leaders must set challenging goals for results and the behaviors that enable them—and then hold themselves accountable for achieving them. Results include objective measures such as numbers of women, people of color, and LGBTQ individuals in each stage of the pipeline (new hires, supervisors, managers, executives, etc.), performance ratings, internal promotions, compensation, and attrition. Behaviors include leading-indicator measures such as perceived support, perceived barriers, and desire to advance.

## Know your goal

When we experience injustice, we often feel provoked and disrespected—even angry. Before you speak up, think about what you really want to have happen. Do you want an apology, punishment, repentance? Is it enough for the bad behavior to stop? What kind of relationship would you like? The clearer your goals, the more likely you are to achieve them.

**Identify crucial moments.** Locate the times, places, and circumstances when bias is most likely to occur. For example, identify the crucial moments in a:

- **Career path.** Job search, interviews, reviews, job opportunities, assignments, development, and promotions
- **Life path.** Marriage, pregnancy, adoption, childcare, eldercare, sickness, and relocation
- **Daily work environment.** Poor performance on an assignment, good performance on an assignment, friction with managers, harassment, and an obnoxious coworker

**Combine diverse solutions.** Most diversity and inclusion initiatives employ a single solution—training programs, specific policies, or support from the top. Our research shows that combining four or more solutions makes initiatives 10 times more likely to succeed.[1]

## State your take

Skilled individuals are careful to describe their concerns absent the judgments and accusations the rest of us hold when we speak up. For example, replace "What you said about my pregnancy was sexist and abusive" with "Last Friday you said, 'That's the last time I ever hire a woman.'" Describe what really happened—no apologies, no self-repression, no accusations, and no indictments.

Begin with the detailed facts, explain what the facts mean to you, and then invite others to a dialogue where you both can learn.

## Make it safe

Is a person who exhibits unconscious bias automatically a bigot? If so, then we're all bigots. Skilled individuals recognize that what we're up against is a human condition, not simply personal flaws. It's challenging to describe biased behavior without making others feel attacked. Achieving a better outcome for the future requires that we help others and ourselves feel safe while addressing uncomfortable issues. For example, you might begin with, "I don't think you realize how that came across . . ."

Bias—especially unintentional, unconscious bias—is a stubborn problem, one deeply rooted in our culture. Eradicating it is exceptionally tough, and individuals should not feel a responsibility to change that culture on their own. But by following these suggestions, they can make small changes to respond better when faced with bias and take steps in the right direction.

*Adapted from "How to React to Biased Comments at Work," on hbr.org, May 3, 2017 (product #H03MVZ).*

15

# When People Assume You're Not in Charge Because You're a Woman

by Amy Diehl and Leanne M. Dzubinski

When a digital marketer we'll call Alexandra attended meetings alone, clients often asked, "Are we waiting for him to arrive?" "Him" was an imaginary person, Alexandra's supposed male boss. The clients assumed that Alexandra was in a support role instead of the key decision maker.

For a while Alexandra downplayed the mistake for fear of offending the clients, but soon she realized that their condescending view limited discussions. As she explained, "Walking into a negotiation where the other person is basically telling you up front they deem you less than, even before you open your mouth, was and is demoralizing."

Alexandra's experience isn't unique. Many women have faced similar assumptions about their positions in their organization. We propose a new term for this behavior: role incredulity.

Role incredulity is a form of gender bias where women are mistakenly assumed to be in a support or stereotypically female role—secretary, administrative assistant, court reporter, nurse, wife, girlfriend—rather than a leadership or stereotypically male role, such as CEO, professor, lawyer, doctor, or engineer. In these instances, women must expend extra energy and time to assert and sometimes prove their credentials, as people may think they lack the credibility and authority inherent in their position. Role incredulity surfaced as a common theme in our research data set of women's stories from interviews, open-ended survey responses, social media posts, and public articles.

Many women on Twitter have expressed frustration with role incredulity. Some women were flat-out told they don't look like someone in a male-dominated role ("You don't look like an engineer") or were received incredulously.[1] For instance, one woman was introduced to a colleague's male friend, and the friend expressed surprise that she was a reporter, explaining that he assumed the women were in the newsroom "to type up the stories for the men."[2] Role incredulity can even be a safety issue: A geomicrobiologist was injured in her own lab when a young male staff member wouldn't listen to her.[3]

Women of color frequently find themselves subjected to role incredulity. On Twitter, several medical doctors described being mistaken for the wife or girlfriend of a physician, as Dr. Uché Blackstock noted: "For the umpteenth time, I was asked again today by a parking garage attendant (while looking at my MD license plate for hospital parking), 'Are you the doctor or is your husband?'"[4] Similarly, at a fellowship welcome picnic, Dr. Jennifer Huang was mistakenly assumed to be another fellow's girlfriend or wife, and Dr. Nancy Yen Shipley was assumed to be the wife of a medical doctor at a fellowship interview.[5] Dr. Yen Shipley commented, "I mean, I'm a wife. Of someone else. Who is not at the fellowship mixer."

Role incredulity can even happen to women working in positions that aren't male-dominated. Author Kalani Pickhart works in a university staff role. She shared that when faculty members find out that she is publishing a novel, "You can see their brain short-circuit like, 'Wait, you're not supposed to be capable of anything but making my copies.'"[6] In another example, a cosmetologist has had clients request a male employee do their makeup because "those types are just so much better."

Role incredulity is harmful for both individuals and organizations. Not only must women manage their emotions while being doubted repeatedly and expend extra time and energy to assert their roles, but the assumptions can also hamper their career paths. In situations where evaluations may be based on timely responses, such as in customer service or technical support, a woman's ratings may be lower simply because she must spend time defending her expertise before she can attend to the customer's problem. When women are not seen as a leader, an engineer, or a physician in the same way that men are, they may be less likely to be hired into male-dominated roles or to be considered for promotions. Within organizations, role incredulity serves to maintain gender inequity and thwarts the benefits of having an inclusive workforce. When only a certain profile or type of employee (typically a white male) is seen as capable of expressing authority or exercising leadership, the organization misses out on the wisdom and perspectives of underrepresented groups—perspectives that have been shown to increase organizational performance.[7]

But organizational leaders, workplace allies, and women themselves can take steps to prevent and correct role incredulity. Here are a few we've seen in our work that can help.

## Set Norms

First, organizational leaders can model equality and set norms for the rest of the organization, using practices to help curtail role incredulity. Such practices could include:

- Making name and title introductions standard in all settings in which individuals may not know each other well

- Using auto-generated signatures in company email systems that include names, position titles, and credentials
- Announcing promotions over companywide email and introducing those who are promoted with their new titles in all meetings for a set period of time
- Instituting a culture where everyone wears a name tag or an ID badge that includes their position title
- Adding position titles to the name display on web conferencing platforms, and issuing nameplates with position titles for desks and door labels in physical offices

Additionally, be aware of how your organization is signaling roles in its communications. Use images of people of all races and genders in various positions in promotional materials, and make sure your company is living into these representations in its promotion and hiring practices. For example, in a medical environment, images on the walls and websites could show men in nursing roles and women in physician roles and include people of varying races, ethnicities, and ages, reflecting the reality of the organization. And if professional titles (Dr., Rev., Coach, Professor, etc.) are used with names, use them for everyone. Untitling women while using professional titles for men is another way that role incredulity is perpetuated.

## Be an Ally

As a boss or colleague, step in to emphasize the roles women have in your organization. When introducing female colleagues, include their title: "I'd like you to meet Hailey Williams, our chief operating officer." If you hear your coworker's role misidentified, speak up on their behalf: "Hannah is serving as the lead architect for this project." One woman's male subordinate came up with a solution for informal settings to avoid the mistaken assumption that he was in charge: "In public, he frequently addressed me as 'boss' rather than my name."[8]

While initially it can feel awkward or embarrassing to call attention to others' mistakes—or your own (see the sidebar, "Own Your Mistakes")—don't let that stop you. If an introduction was not made, put the blame on yourself: "I'm sorry. I forgot to introduce you to Julie Lewis, our company president." Or blame an external factor, such as stress or a change, for a colleague's misstep: "Darryl, there've been a lot of changes this past year. Perhaps you didn't realize that Samantha is now the director of sales. She'll be explaining the current situation to us today."

As a woman, if you're frequently in situations where your role isn't acknowledged, develop a buddy system with a fellow woman to emphasize your titles. Going into the meeting, each of you can introduce the other: "This is Dr. Smith, dean of the science college." "And this is Dr. Jones, chair of the chemistry department."

### Own Your Mistakes

If you make a mistake about someone's role, don't just laugh it off or ignore it. Apologize and own it: "I'm so sorry, Dr. Davis, please forgive me." But don't stop there; learn from it. Moving forward, work twice as hard to ensure you know people's qualifications and roles. Do your homework in advance of meetings, conference calls, or events to learn who will be attending and ensure you know their positions and titles. Doing so will help you to prevent incorrect assumptions, offer an opportunity for you to step in and introduce or correct others, and set a good example.

## Proactively Identify Your Role

While the steps above will help in the long run, in the short term many women will still find that they're in situations where role incredulity rears its ugly head. In those instances, include your position title and credentials in your email signature and web conferencing platforms, and introduce yourself with your title in settings with new people and those you don't know well. Don't wait for someone to make the introduction for you: "Hi, I'm Dr. Harris, your surgeon" or "Hello, I'm Kiana Green, the chief financial officer of the company. Today I'll be presenting the current budget numbers and the projections for the coming fiscal year."

If your role is misidentified, politely correct the misinformed person: “Actually, I’m the lawyer/physician/president/director.” Here humor or a light touch can be helpful: “I’ve been doing this work for over 10 years, and I’m pretty good at it.” Most often role incredulity is not intentional, and it can be helpful to educate others about our titles and positions. While it’s not an excuse, customers, patients, and clients are often just acting on ingrained stereotypes. Informing others of your role can help to reduce these biases and assumptions. When one surgeon informed her patient’s husband of his role incredulity, he changed his tone, saying, “Thank you, ma’am, for everything.”[9]

These solutions may seem superficial when the problem with role incredulity is systemic. But by taking steps to change workplace norms, we will slowly but surely promote gender equity in attitudes and stereotypes.

*Adapted from content posted on hbr.org, December 22, 2021 (product #H06RDQ).*

16

# Your Boss Made a Biased Remark—Now What?

by Aneeta Rattan

When I ask my MBA students if they would respond to a biased remark at work, there's a unanimous response: Everybody says yes, they would. But when I ask them how they'd react to the same comment from their boss, I usually hear, "I would still want to speak up. But I wouldn't know how to actually do it."

They are not alone. Research shows that people have a hard time standing up to biased comments from someone more powerful than them.[1] When you are the only person in the room who comes from a certain background, it's even harder. Sometimes your colleagues and peers may even fail to acknowledge that the comment was biased at all.

If you ever find yourself in this situation, first of all, know this: No matter how conscious or unconscious a bias is, it hurts. You're not overreacting; you are just reacting. It's OK to feel angry, confused, overwhelmed, or disappointed. Whatever you feel is valid.

You should also know that, realistically, there are some situations in which you face real risks in confronting the person in power about their behavior. Perhaps you have a toxic boss. Perhaps your job security matters more to you right now than addressing their comment. Perhaps you're not in the right frame of mind to speak out about it. Or maybe you just don't have the energy, bandwidth, or emotional resources to do so. All of these are OK.

In the heat of the moment, take a deep breath. Pause. Then, ask yourself: "How would I behave if a friend failed to confront their boss's biased comment?" You'd likely be sympathetic and help them see why they should not blame themselves or feel guilty about their (non)action, right? Be that friend to yourself. Look after yourself. That's what matters most.

## Learning to Speak Up

That said, if you do choose to address your boss's biased comment, it's important to understand when to bring it up and how to communicate your discomfort.

One of the trickiest things about speaking up is choosing the right time. I get asked this question a lot: Should you speak out in the moment or start a conversation later? Is there a way to make this less awkward and more effective?

It depends on two things: Your boss and the nature of the bias.

If your boss is someone who values equality and strives to be inclusive, or if you immediately notice that others are offended, then speaking up in the moment is likely to work better. Ironically, given how unexpected these moments of bias are, being ready to speak up requires a bit of preparation on your end. You need to be ready with strong opening and closing statements.

Given how jarring it can be to hear a biased comment at work, it's a good idea to have a few rehearsed phrases that can help you feel grounded even in that awful moment. These statements will help you express your disagreement in a practiced way, minimizing the chance that your boss will feel labeled or attacked.

Ask questions that express your discomfort but also probe the other person to rethink what they just said. Here are some examples I recommend:

- "What specifically did you mean by that, because I'm not sure I got it."
- "That could be taken wrong—can you explain what you meant?"
- "That's not OK with me, and I respect you enough to let you know."

Don't bother with a verbal back-and-forth where one attacks and the other defends. Draw your boss's attention to what they said, its implications, and how it made you feel. Being brief, straightforward, and probing gives the other party an opportunity to realize the bias they expressed, own it, quickly step back from the comment, and apologize.

You should then end the conversation with a closing statement that conveys what you want them to understand or do moving forward: Do you want your boss to behave more appropriately? Do you want them to educate themself? Whatever your end goal is, ask for it. Then, endorse your boss's ability to grow, learn, and change. You can say:

- "I hope you understand now the negative impact your words had on me."
- "I hope you'll reconsider your assumptions on this issue."
- "Can I ask you not to say that around me again?"

Any of these can be followed by, "I'm telling you this because I believe, when it comes to issues of bias, we can all learn and grow." If your boss is genuinely interested in hearing you out, your conversation can help them redeem themself. (For a firsthand account of someone who spoke up, see the sidebar, "Witnessing Bias: An Example.")

## Witnessing Bias: An Example

**BY CARMEN ACTON**

My first stint as a manager was in the safety engineering department of an energy company. I was the youngest of three supervisors, and a few months in, I found myself sequestered in a brightly lit conference room with my manager and two peers for a team appraisal meeting.

We were each tasked with evaluating the performance of our respective team members. Once we assessed and agreed upon the high-performing team members, it was time to discuss the performance of those who hadn't consistently met our expectations.

"I've rated Karla as below expectations," Ben said.

I was surprised. Although Karla was Ben's direct report, she had worked closely with my team on many big projects. She'd consistently delivered on our goals and was a strong team player. I was curious to know how Ben had reached his decision, but being the youngest and newest manager in the room, I was hesitant to bring it up.

I took a few deep breaths and went for it.

"What I have observed, and heard from my team, is that Karla always delivers timely and quality reports. My team wouldn't have been able to do their job without her support. I'm curious to know what you've

*(continued)*

noticed that would put her in the below expectations category, Ben."

"She missed a deadline on a critical report for the vice president. I had to step in to get it done."

To my knowledge, the incident Ben was referring to was a last-minute request (and a time-consuming one at that). It had required Karla to learn a completely new software program and was a single instance of failure—albeit an important one.

I probed further. "Was Karla familiar with the software program required to complete the task? Did she have all the data necessary at hand?" More specifically, I wanted to know if there was any other evidence of Karla missing deadlines or delivering incomplete work.

What Ben said next shook me.

"Don't worry, Karla probably won't be staying here that long." He let out a slow, dismissive sigh. "She has two kids, and her husband works. Besides, she's only working part-time anyway."

My stomach somersaulted. I could feel the heat rising in my neck. *What does Karla's personal life have to do with her performance?* I almost retorted. There were several employees on our team with families. And what was up with his tone?

I wondered if I was the only one baffled by his words. *Am I reading too much into this? Should I let it go? Should I wait for a one-on-one or should I speak up now?*

Karla was a college-educated woman and mother of two. She was a woman of color—in fact, the only one on our team of more than 20 employees. Working part-time was an accepted practice at our company.

The longer the silence was prolonged, the more I felt compelled to share my thoughts. After all, the goal of the meeting was to leave in agreement on the overall team evaluation, and I wasn't in agreement.

I took a leap.

I pointed out that Karla's personal decisions had nothing to do with her performance. Our job, as supervisors, was to look at an employee's performance against the goals set for them. Thankfully, our boss agreed and said we needed to take the time to discuss each employee's contributions and not allow assumptions or potential biases to cloud our evaluation. The ultimate outcome was a decision that everyone agreed with and supported.

Adapted from "Don't Be Afraid to Stand Up for What's Right," Ascend, on hbr.org, September 7, 2021.

If you're of the view that people can change, then speaking up also benefits you. In research I conducted with psychologist Carol Dweck, we found that people who both believed in others' ability to change and imagined confronting (or actually had confronted) the person who expressed bias reported a relatively less negative outlook toward the person. This, in turn, was associated with them retaining more of their sense of satisfaction and belonging in the workplace.[2]

In cases where you're not really sure what your boss values or how they will react to you, or if you're in front of a client, a senior leader, or a big group of people, wait to bring up the issue in private. Then, proceed by following the steps already described.

Of course, it's possible that your boss will double down on their biased comments and go after you for addressing it. Remember that you are not powerless, and you are not in the wrong. If you know your boss to be someone who is deeply biased, and you don't want to confront them alone, your best option is to write an email instead. State the facts of what was said, what made you uncomfortable, and how you disagree with them. In this way, you are documenting the situation, should the bias escalate. You can also reach out to other senior leaders you trust, a mentor if you have one, or the HR team in your company.

While calling people out can genuinely prompt some to realize their mistakes and change, know that you're not obligated to speak up. It's not your job to teach others about discrimination and marginalization; it's their job to learn. All you can do is tell them that it may be time to start their learning journey.

*Adapted from "Your Boss Made a Biased Remark. Should You Confront Them?" Ascend, on hbr.org, December 22, 2020.*

SECTION SIX

# Build a Better Culture—Together

17

# Leaders, Stop Denying the Gender Inequity in Your Organization

by Michelle King

The lack of women in leadership is not simply an issue of representation. Focusing solely on getting more women into leadership positions, at the expense of other related factors, not only treats women as token hires but also excludes men, who are made to feel as though prioritizing diversity and inclusion is a win-lose fight for a seat at the table. And improving representation will not, on its own, fix the culture and environment that excluded women in the first place.

Rather, the real aim should be for leaders to create a culture that values, rewards, and supports individual differences. In a work environment where differences are valued, everyone has an opportunity to advance, which is why both women and men are more likely to rise to senior leadership positions.

So why aren't leaders creating these environments? In a word, denial. While most people know that women have different experiences than men at work, I found in my research that a majority of leaders are in denial about that fact. I interviewed 72 men and women from two different organizations. These senior executives consistently upheld the belief that workplaces are meritocracies and that all employees are treated in the same way. Almost every one of my interviewees said that they believed men and women have identical opportunities, workplace experiences, and career paths. Consequently, they believed that women do not succeed because of their individual choices or capabilities, not because of unwelcoming and even hostile work environments.

Most workplaces were created by men and for men, which in turn has created numerous challenges for women to overcome. The situation only gets worse when leaders make public commitments to increase the number of women in leadership roles and then continue to rely on ineffective solutions as the means to achieving this. Leaders might be aware that there is a gender equality problem, but very few understand how inequality works. (See the sidebar, "Bias Persists in Female-Dominated Workplaces.")

Leaders set the standards for behavior in organizations. They decide what gets endorsed, accepted, supported,

## Bias Persists in Female-Dominated Workplaces

BY AMY DIEHL, AMBER L. STEPHENSON, AND LEANNE M. DZUBINSKI

It's been thought that once industries achieve gender balance, bias will decrease and gender gaps will close. People often assume that having more women present is all that's needed to promote change—the "add women and stir" approach. But simply adding women into a workplace does not change the organizational structures and systems that benefit men more than women. Our research shows gender bias is still prevalent in gender-balanced and female-dominated industries.[1]

That research examines gender bias in four industries with more female than male workers: law, higher education, faith-based nonprofits, and health care. Using the Gender Bias Scale along with open-ended questions, we compared perceptions and experiences of gender bias for 1,606 women leaders in these fields across 15 factors, ranging from subtle (such as lack of acknowledgement) to overt (such as workplace harassment).

Even though women are the majority in these industries, we found they still experience a multitude of biases. One example is constrained communication,

*(continued)*

in which women must be mindful when expressing authority and downplay their accomplishments. They also report a lack of acknowledgement for their contributions and being interrupted by men when speaking. And even when women were well represented, their workplace often still had a boys' club mentality, with decisions being made mostly by men. The participants were at times on a glass cliff, held responsible for problems outside of their control. They often lacked mentors and sponsors. And lastly, some women found no other choice but to limit their aspirations due to personal obligations. In other words, their workplace was not supportive of combining work with family.

Having balanced or even greater numbers of women in an organization is not, by itself, changing women's experiences of bias. Bias is built into the system and continues to operate even when more women than men are present.

Adapted from "Research: How Bias Against Women Persists in Female-Dominated Workplaces," on hbr.org, March 2, 2022 (product #H06UXD).

overlooked, and rewarded. They decide how many women will be on a team, and more importantly if they will be treated in a way that enables them to thrive in the organization. A policy or training program can't compensate for leaders who consistently ignore or even endorse toxic behaviors, such as comments or jokes that discriminate against, marginalize, or exclude women.

Inclusion does or doesn't happen in millions of moments each day, and leaders need to stop denying the reality for women and become aware of all the ways they enable inequality to unfold in their teams.

The call for leaders to advance gender equality at work, regardless of whether they lead a startup, a multinational, or a public-sector organization, is in reality an invitation for them to lead. Here's how they can do that.

## Disrupt Denial

The first step is for leaders to get out of denial and become aware of how inequality shows up in their team, department, and organization. Even if they are aware of the barriers, they can help others pay more attention. To do so, they must create opportunities for employees to talk about their experiences of marginalization and discrimination. One leader at a large multinational organization that I spoke with as part of my research held an hour-long weekly meeting with their teams to openly discuss topics like the pay gap, the motherhood penalty, and microaggressions to raise awareness of the barriers women face, the impact those barriers have, and what needs to be done to tackle these issues. While discussing these topics might make some leaders uncomfortable at first, it is important to lean into this discomfort, as this is how we make invisible experiences of inequality visible.

## Get to Know the Barriers

How many leaders understand the barriers women face at work? Start with the fact that women must perform at a higher standard than men to achieve the same level of success. This performance tax limits women's pay and promotion opportunities.[2] There's also the role conflict that many women encounter as they try to manage the often incompatible roles of worker, wife, and mother.[3] And many women experience identity conflict when trying to lead in workplaces where only masculine management styles are recognized and rewarded.[4] It's important for leaders to know that every one of these challenges is made harder still when women have multiple intersecting identities due to race, ethnicity, sexual orientation, physical or mental ability, religion, and age.

It's not enough to be aware that there is a problem, and it's certainly not enough to throw a quota or another training initiative into place, which requires no real effort from leaders. To solve inequality, we need leaders to educate themselves by reading about, researching, and understanding why these challenges exist, as well as to thoughtfully consider how, as leaders, they might be unknowingly creating or upholding such barriers.

## Manage the Moments

Inequality is a practice—it's something people do, which is why leaders need to continuously manage behaviors that cause inequality in the same way that they manage safety, costs, and productivity. It doesn't matter how many policies or diversity and inclusion initiatives are in place if leaders and employees cannot translate equality into a set of behaviors, norms, and routines.

This means leaders should call out inappropriate or exclusionary behaviors, especially when they happen in informal interactions; give employees direct one-on-one feedback outlining how their behavior marginalizes other employees (whether intentionally or not); and explain the impact these moments have on the team. They should not, as too many leaders do, ignore the incident or downplay its impact in the hope that it will go away. The most committed leaders can also use these experiences as opportunities for collective learning with their teams by sharing what happened and what will change as a result. When leaders do this on a regular basis, they raise employees' awareness of the problem and encourage everyone to solve the issue by changing their behavior.

Even though managing discrimination can be challenging for leaders, it's a lot harder for employees to work in an environment where their identity is devalued. Being in a position to tackle inequality that you yourself may never have to experience is the ultimate privilege.

There are more inclusion initiatives than ever before, from diversity targets to focused recruitment efforts, unconscious bias training, and individual development programs for women, which often include mentoring, sponsorship, and coaching. With all this activity, it's easy to assume progress is being made. But none of these efforts will guarantee that women reach management positions or that, when they do, they'll be valued in the same way as men. That's where leaders come in. It's on the most powerful people in the organization to set the standard for the types of behaviors they want employees to adopt and to give them the skills and feedback they need to practice equality as part of their day-to-day job—so it becomes a fundamental way of working. That's the only way organizations will become truly equal.

*Adapted from content posted on hbr.org, June 19, 2020 (product #H05OWA).*

# 18

# Break Up Your Masculinity Contest Culture

by Jennifer L. Berdahl, Peter Glick, and Marianne Cooper

From Uber to Nike to CBS, exposés have revealed dysfunctional workplaces rife with misconduct, bullying, and sexual harassment. Why do companies get caught up in illegal behavior, harassment, and toxic leadership?

Our research identifies an underlying cause: what we call a "masculinity contest culture." This kind of culture endorses winner-take-all competition, where winners demonstrate stereotypically masculine traits such as emotional toughness, physical stamina, and ruthlessness. It produces organizational dysfunction, as employees become hypercompetitive to win.

## Masculinity Contest Cultures

We surveyed thousands of workers in the United States and Canada from different organizations. Respondents rated whether various masculine qualities were highly prized in their workplace; they also reported on other organizational characteristics and their personal outcomes. Four masculine norms, which together define masculinity contest cultures, emerged as highly correlated with each other and with organizational dysfunction:

1. **"Show no weakness."** A workplace that demands swaggering confidence, never admitting doubt or mistakes, and suppressing any tender or vulnerable emotions ("no sissy stuff")

2. **"Strength and stamina."** A workplace that prizes strong or athletic people (even in white-collar work) or those who show off their endurance (e.g., by working extreme hours)

3. **"Put work first."** A workplace where nothing outside the organization (e.g., family) can interfere with work, and where taking a break or a leave represents an impermissible lack of commitment

4. **"Dog eat dog."** A workplace filled with ruthless competition, where "winners" (the more masculine) focus on defeating "losers" (the less masculine) and no one is trusted

These norms take root in organizations because behaving in accordance with them is what makes someone a "man." As phrases like "man up" illustrate, *being* a man is something men must prove—not just once, but repeatedly. In many cultures around the world, someone becomes a "man" by behaving in ways that conform with cultural beliefs about what men are like—dominant, tough, risk-taking, aggressive, and rule-breaking.

And it doesn't take much to make men feel like "less of a man." Men react defensively when they even just *think* about job loss or when they receive feedback suggesting they have a "feminine" personality.[1]

What all of this means is that masculinity is precarious: hard-won and easily lost. And the need to repeatedly prove their manhood can lead men to behave aggressively, take unwarranted risks, work extreme hours, engage in cutthroat competition, and sexually harass women (or other men), especially when they feel a masculinity threat.[2]

At work, this pressure to prove "I have what it takes" shifts the focus from accomplishing the organization's mission to proving one's masculinity. The result: endless "mine's bigger than yours" contests, such as taking on and bragging about heavy workloads or long hours, cutting corners to outearn others, and taking unreasonable risks either physically (in blue-collar jobs) or in decision making (e.g., rogue traders in finance).[3] The competition breeds unspoken anxiety (because admitting anxiety is seen as weak) and defensiveness (e.g., blaming subordinates for any failure), undermining cooperation, psychological safety, trust in coworkers, and the ability to admit uncertainty or mistakes. Together this creates miserable, counterproductive work environments that increase stress, burnout, and turnover.

Masculinity contests are most prevalent—and vicious—in male-dominated occupations where extreme and precarious resources are at stake. Think about finance and tech startups, where billions of dollars are quickly made or lost; surgery, where high-stakes operations leave no room for error; and military and police units, where risky jobs are performed under strict chains of command.

Where does this leave women? Like everyone else, women must try to play the game to survive, and the few who succeed may do so by behaving just as badly as the men vying to win. But the game is rigged against women and minorities: Suspected of not "having what it takes," they must work harder to prove themselves while facing backlash for displaying dominant behaviors like anger and self-promotion. Women and minorities thus face a double bind that makes them less likely to succeed; they may find it easier to survive by playing supporting roles to men who are winning the contest.

## Changing Masculinity Contest Cultures

Despite being toxic, masculinity contest cultures persist for two reasons:

1. The association between toxic masculinity and success is so strong that people feel compelled to keep playing the game, despite the dysfunctional behavior it produces.

2. Questioning the masculinity contest marks one as a "loser," which disincentivizes people from pushing back.

Dropping a diversity initiative onto these types of workplaces is unlikely to create meaningful change. In fact, current interventions, like those to prevent sexual harassment, typically fail or even backfire in these environments (by creating more harassment).[4] Real change requires shutting down the game.

To accomplish this, organizations need to perform deeper, more committed work to examine and diagnose their cultures. These efforts must be led by those who have the power to spark serious reform. It is crucial to generate awareness of the masculinity contest and its role in creating organizational problems. For instance, people tend to attribute sexual harassment to "a few bad apples," ignoring how an organization's culture unleashed, allowed, and even may have rewarded the misconduct. When organizations do not tolerate bullying and harassment, the bad apples are kept in check and good apples do not go bad.

Two specific actions are a good place to start:

## Establish a stronger focus on the organization's mission

Current trainings backfire, in part, because they focus on compliance and what not to do, are often framed as trying to make things better for women and minorities rather than for everyone, and seem unconnected to the organization's core mission. Effective interventions require authentic and meaningful connections to core organizational values and goals.

For example, researchers have documented how an energy company undermined masculinity contest norms on oil rigs through a safety intervention.[5] The bottom line demanded reform: Oil rig disasters cost lives and money and result in environmental destruction, legal liability, and severe reputational damage. Leaders convinced workers that increased safety was central to the mission, and they monitored and rewarded desired behavior change. Workers were rewarded for voicing doubts or uncertainties about a procedure (rather than "showing no weakness"), for listening to each other (rather than obeying the "strongest" alpha male), for valuing safety and taking breaks (rather than "putting work first"), and for cooperating with and caring for coworkers (rather than engaging in "dog eat dog" competition). The need to prove one's manhood proved incompatible with the new mission-based rules. Not only were accidents and injuries reduced, but so were bullying, harassment, burnout, and stress.

Organizations can leverage other core goals to motivate reform. Given the inherent dysfunctionality that masculinity contest cultures create, chances are that almost any mission-related reform can help. For example, research has found a common characteristic among innovative teams: psychological safety.[6] Team members know that they can raise questions or voice doubts without eliciting ridicule or rejection. An initiative to foster innovation via greater psychological safety would naturally dampen the masculinity contest. As a by-product, the work environment should become more hospitable and inclusive toward women and minorities; after all, whose ideas are most often summarily ignored or dismissed in masculinity contest cultures?

## Dispel misconceptions that "everyone endorses this"

People fail to question masculinity contest norms lest they be tagged as a whiny, soft loser. As a result, everyone goes along to get along, publicly reinforcing norms they privately hate: People stay late just to be seen as putting work first, or laugh at a joke they actually think is offensive. Because people *publicly* uphold the norms, it appears as though everyone endorses them. Research has shown that people in masculinity contest cultures *think* their coworkers embrace these norms when in fact they do not, breeding pervasive but silent dissatisfaction alongside active complicity as people stay quiet to prove they belong.[7]

Leaders can remedy this misperception by publicly rejecting masculinity contest norms and empowering others to voice their previously secret dissent. But they also need to walk the talk by changing reward systems, modeling new behavior, and punishing the misconduct that was previously overlooked or rewarded. Additionally, leaders need to ensure that people who speak up are not punished or retaliated against for doing so, either formally (e.g., with job consequences) or informally (e.g., by reputation and ostracism).

When masculinity contest cultures become "the way business gets done," both organizations and the people within them suffer. Solving the problem requires meaningful commitment to culture change—to creating a work environment in which mission takes precedence over masculinity.

*Adapted from "How Masculinity Contests Undermine Organizations, and What to Do About It," on hbr.org, November 2, 2018 (product #H04MT0).*

# 19

# Male Allyship Is About Paying Attention

by W. Brad Johnson and David G. Smith

Although most men notionally support gender inclusion and equity, there is clear research that men often struggle to recognize gender discrimination and harassment in real time. For instance, despite the #MeToo movement's focus on workplace sexual harassment and assault, a 2018 study revealed that 77% of men didn't see harassment as a problem—even as 38% of their female colleagues reported experiencing workplace harassment.[1] Lack of awareness can keep even well-intentioned men on the sidelines, rather than serving as effective advocates and accomplices for change.[2]

Situational awareness is a key element of what we refer to as male gender intelligence (GQ). Sharpening your situational awareness requires greater vigilance in noticing the gender dynamics operating in the workplace.

Developing more acute situational awareness demands that men focus on the relational environment, watch carefully, ask curious questions of female colleagues, and engage in generous listening. Moreover, it requires honest humility and a perpetual learning orientation. Situationally aware men become more acutely attuned to gender inequities and harassment and are more willing to address them in real time.

How can an aspiring male ally begin to sharpen his situational awareness and increase his GQ? Amy Orlov of Forté Foundation recommends that men "look for patterns and begin to notice workplace behavior and dynamics they didn't even see before. What is happening in the room? How are your female colleagues experiencing this moment? Try to objectively observe these dynamics."

Here are several things men can begin doing today to build their awareness of women's experiences and gender inequities in the workplace.

## Self-Educate

Self-education heightens awareness of gender inequities, reduces sexist attitudes, and increases participation in gender equity initiatives.[3] Build your own GQ by reading about gender in the workplace and attending gender inclusion events. In the words of inclusion consultant Jennifer

Brown, "Emotional labor is part of allyship. An ally takes the time to do their homework in reading, listening, understanding, without burdening women or people of color to do more of the labor they've been doing already."

## Attend to Nonverbals

Building better situational awareness requires improving your skill at reading nonverbal language. Be aware of any nonverbal signals that all is not well with a female colleague. In one of her first jobs as a reporter, Gretchen Carlson was sexually harassed by a photographer assigned to a news story with her. She recalled, "The news director at the time saw that I was distressed and having trouble focusing on the story I was writing. He kept coming up to me and asking, 'What's wrong?' He was perceptive enough to notice something was wrong, kind enough to care about it, and I eventually told him what had happened." He relieved the photographer of his duties immediately.

To be more situationally aware, consider the following questions as you go about your day:

- How would you describe the mood in the room (e.g., good-natured, energized, icy, angry, anxious)?
- Who appears to be comfortable? Who is folded in on themselves?

- Who's clenching their jaw or furrowing their brow (classic signs of stress)?
- Who's not laughing at a joke along with others?
- Who's avoiding making eye contact?
- When the norm in the virtual environment is to have cameras on, who keeps their camera off?

## Notice Sexist Words and Phrases

Be attuned to sexist comments, biased language, and even overt, leering harassment. Sift the ambient noise, the side conversations, banter, and formal dialogue. Actively listen for those daily slights, objectifying comments, and stereotypes that leave women feeling inferior or unsafe. Situationally aware male allies quickly debug conversations so that they can efficiently disrupt bias and call out misogyny. Ask yourself:

- Do you hear condescending or patronizing language? Who is the target?
- Are sexual innuendos or inappropriate humor often heard in the context of "bro banter"?
- Are women in the room visibly uncomfortable with the topic or something that's been said?

## Focus on the Intersections

Developing your GQ and sharpening your situational awareness requires learning about the experiences of women of color (among other intersectional identities). Understand and notice that they are more likely than white women to feel devalued, demeaned, disrespected, excluded, and isolated. Many women of color feel invisible because they are not the dominant group for either their gender or their race.[4] A situationally aware man is more inclined to notice when a Black woman is held to an unfair standard, overlooked for a promotion opportunity, offered less money at hiring, or mistaken for administrative or janitorial staff—and he's more likely to intervene. Here are some questions to ask yourself:

- Do you notice simplified language or assumptions that define people by a single identity?
- Do people on your team avoid conversations about identities different from their own?
- Are there people who are more likely to "cover" or hide their identities because they don't feel comfortable or safe expressing them?

## Pay Attention to Who Is Included

One in five women report being the only woman in the room at work. Senior-level women and those in male-dominated professions are twice as likely to have this experience. "Only" women are also 50% more likely to consider quitting.[5] Joanne Lipman, former editor in chief of *USA Today*, reminds men that women in male-centric environments can experience *belonging uncertainty*: "You are not invited to lunch or drinks with the guys and don't feel comfortable inviting yourself. When you walk into a meeting, the guys are already in there doing their premeeting, talking to each other, laughing . . . and then they go silent when you walk in." Notice who is included—and who is not—and go out of your way to make female colleagues feel that they belong. Ask yourself:

- Who's in the meeting? Who is missing?
- Given the topic of discussion, who should be present to discuss their work or serve as a subject-matter expert? Do the attendees match that list?
- If the meeting is in person, who's sitting at the table? Who's standing or sitting in an outer ring?
- Who's speaking most of the time, and who rarely contributes? Whose input hasn't been solicited, and who is being ignored?
- Who's being interrupted? Who's being dismissed?

## Ask Women About Their Experiences

Validate what you've learned through the lived experiences of women with whom you've created trusting relationships. Often, a humble and curious question goes a long way toward building better empathy and situational awareness. Many women we interviewed in our research emphasized the importance of asking. Ipek Serifsoy, president of the Deep Coaching Institute, said, "Men have a terrible time fathoming the things women experience daily. Women are reluctant to share negative experiences with men because they know on some level that men don't share those experiences. So, men need to be humble and acknowledge there's a lot they don't understand." Here are some examples of good ways to start a conversation:

- "I'm curious about some of the things women in this organization find most challenging on a day-to-day basis, things that I—as a man—might not notice."
- "If there was one thing you wish men who work here were more aware of, something men could do, or stop doing, what would that be?"
- "If there was something I could be more aware of—perhaps one thing I could start doing every day that might make the workplace better for you and other women—what would that be?"

- "If a guy asked how he could really show up as a male ally to make the workplace fairer and more welcoming for women, what would you tell him?"

Developing a deeper understanding of the experiences of the women around you and sharpening your situational awareness will inevitably and irrevocably transform your perspective. Asking, listening, and learning in this way will benefit everything you do as an ally, as a leader, and as a man. One man who took the time to really ask about the experiences of his female colleagues reflected: "Once you put on that lens, you can't take it off. The world never looks the same."[6]

*Adapted from content posted on hbr.org, February 10, 2021 (product #H0665V).*

# 20

# How One Biotech Company Narrowed the Gender Gap in Its Top Ranks

by Cynthia Burks

In 2007 there were five times as many men as women in officer roles at Genentech, and female directors (the level preceding officers) were leaving at twice the rate as their male counterparts. To achieve equitable representation among men and women in leadership positions and stem the flow of departing talent, we rethought and revised our recruiting, professional development, and succession planning processes. Today, because of those efforts and a top-down commitment to change, men and women are nearly equally represented among our overall employee population and in officer and director roles.

The journey began in 2007 at a town hall meeting, where Art Levinson, who was then Genentech's CEO, drew attention to the shortfall of women moving into our leadership ranks. He shared a table that showed that while the proportions of women and men among all Genentech employees were nearly the same, women accounted for 44% of managers/supervisors, 41% of directors, and a mere 16% of officers. He asked employees, "Do people see what's wrong with this? Is there anyone in this room who can tell me that this is OK? Because it's not."

Inspired by Art's observation and his insistence that we do better, we set a goal for the organization: Identify and remove barriers to the advancement of women to senior leadership positions, and increase the pool of women qualified for such positions by 50%.

In the years that followed, we made earnest, concerted, and consistent efforts to ensure that men and women are equally represented among Genentech's overall employee population and in leadership roles. Along the way, we learned four lessons:

## Data Drives the Process

Genentech is a longtime supporter of the Healthcare Businesswomen's Association (HBA). In 2010 the nonprofit released its landmark E.D.G.E. in Leadership Study, which outlined best practices for recruiting, advancing, and retaining women at pharmaceutical and biotechnology companies. Building on what the HBA study had uncovered, we conducted our own research to pinpoint the obstacles blocking women's paths to success at Genentech.

We applied the same rigor and analysis that we use in scientific research to this process, collecting subjective data (through surveys and focus groups) and objective data (by looking at factors such as the differences between the number of women who applied and were invited to interview for open roles and the number of those women who received and accepted offers). We discovered that women felt they had fewer opportunities than men to take on visible and challenging assignments and that women felt less likely to receive meaningful performance feedback and fair assessments. We also learned they felt their ideas were less likely to be heard and recognized and that they had fewer opportunities to participate in the informal networks that are often key sources of information about what's happening within an organization.

The results of our research underscored what HBA had discovered: Increasing representation required a two-pronged approach of recognizing and growing existing talent and improving our talent pipeline.

## Recognizing and growing existing talent

We had plenty of talented, highly qualified women ready to advance to leadership positions at Genentech, but we weren't doing a good job of recognizing them. To raise their visibility, we held leaders accountable for identifying women on their teams who were primed to move to the next level in their careers and then advocating for them in talent-review discussions where a broader team of leaders could have insight into their potential. The resulting opportunities—to participate in rotational assignments, lead special projects, and cover for more senior colleagues on leave—enabled us to build more thoughtful development and succession plans.

To help women expand their personal and professional support networks, we created the Genentech Women Professionals employee resource group, which hosted career-development events and informal networking activities, and we launched a sponsorship program. Sponsors are senior leaders who act as sounding boards and advocates for the women partnered with them, providing career advice and facilitating connections to other leaders and decision makers throughout the company.

## Improving our talent pipeline

To improve our talent pipeline, we refocused our external sourcing efforts on discovering, attracting, and engaging women candidates. We developed targeted marketing strategies, sponsored and attended conferences geared toward women in science, and joined professional women's associations similar to HBA.

We also redesigned our interview process. Our talent acquisition team assembled a roster of women who volunteered to join interview panels for roles outside their functions. Including at least one woman on interview panels provided candidates with a diversity of perspectives on the Genentech employee experience. And including an interviewer who didn't work on the hiring team helped ensure we were assessing candidates as much on their alignment with Genentech's values, core competencies, and leadership commitments as on the skills and technical expertise they could bring to the role. To remove the risk of groupthink during the debrief process, we implemented an online assessment tool that required interviewers to submit feedback to the hiring manager and recruiter before the panel met to discuss the candidate. These changes helped to reduce bias in our hiring decisions by forcing us to evaluate candidates based on their abilities, rather than on the titles on their résumés and interviewers' assumptions and preferences.

## Everyone Is Accountable

When we launched our gender diversity initiative, we established a baseline against which we could measure our progress year over year. We originally only provided an annual progress update to the board of directors, but we began sharing the data with our employees in 2019.

In 2021 we published our inaugural Diversity & Inclusion Report so that employees, peer companies, and candidates can also hold us accountable.

Accountability is now a critical component of our performance review process. Leaders are expected to create succession plans for their top-performing team members. If there are no women on a leader's list, the leader is expected to explain why—to managers, HR business partners, executive coaches, and our organizational development team. These kinds of conversations, which had never taken place before, proved instrumental in raising awareness of the issue and helping leaders close the gender gaps on their teams. At no point on our journey did we compromise Genentech's high standards to close those gaps; rather, we challenged biases and changed behaviors.

## Small Actions Add Up

The routine tasks we complete day in and day out are ultimately what make science and innovation happen; small steps can add up to something truly life-changing. Weaving the message about the importance of gender diversity into the fabric of our corporate narrative was one small step that made a big difference.

Though Art Levinson was the original champion of our gender diversity efforts, leaders across the organization were equally invested in achieving our goal. At town halls, department meetings, and one-on-ones, they reinforced our commitment to equitable representation and shared updates on our progress. Repetition bred retention, and retention bred habit. Soon all Genentech leaders were actively engaged in the process.

## If You Can't Prove It, It Didn't Happen

As figure 20-1 illustrates, moving the needle on gender diversity at Genentech didn't happen overnight. Making significant change requires shifts in behaviors, perspectives, and processes, and that takes time.

Since 2007 we have more than doubled the percentage of female officers at the company, and by 2017 we achieved our goal of increasing the pool of women qualified for senior leadership positions by 50%.

. . .

Our work is far from done. While the progress we've made on our gender diversity initiative so far is significant, there is still much more to do to create a fully diverse, equitable, and inclusive workplace. Today Genentech's overall employee population is split evenly between people of color and white people, but the gap widens in leadership roles—much as it did between women and men in 2007.

FIGURE 20-1

**Genentech's progress in closing the gender gap in senior leadership roles**

*A breakdown of Genentech's senior management ranks by gender.*

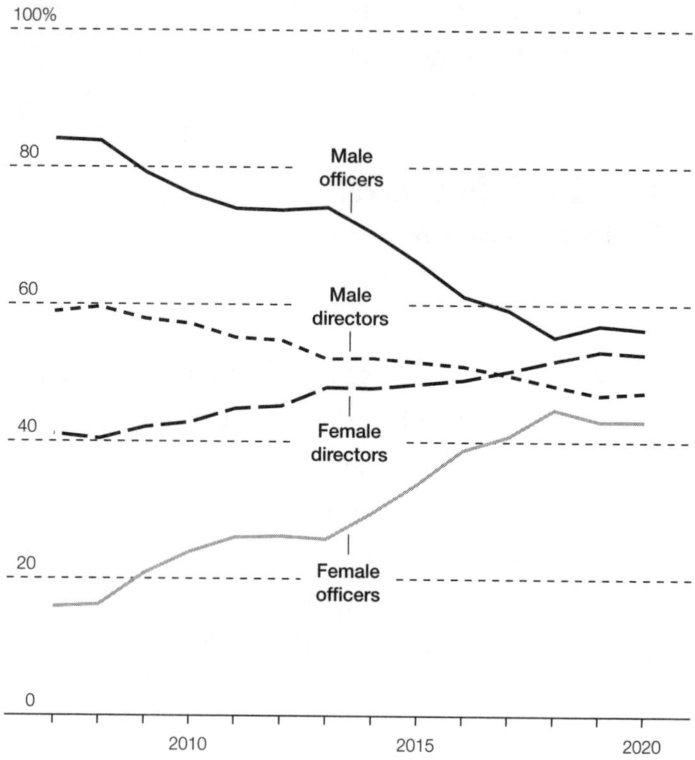


*Source:* Genentech

We've broadened our diversity and inclusion efforts to help ensure that our workforce reflects the increasingly diverse world around us.

An organization that encourages diversity of background, perspective, and experience is far more likely to uncover new insights and unique approaches to addressing a challenge. Diversity is especially vital at Genentech: A broad variety of perspectives and skill sets enhances our ability to discover and develop medicines that treat patients with some of the world's most serious diseases. To that end, attracting and retaining a diverse workforce and giving everyone the opportunity to advance to senior leadership positions is not just a moral and ethical imperative—it's also a critical business priority.

*Adapted from content posted on hbr.org, June 2, 2021 (product #H06DL1).*

# NOTES

## Introduction

1. UN News, "Only 1 in 5 Space Industry Workers Are Women," October 4, 2021, https://news.un.org/en/story/2021/10/1102082.

2. Laura Morgan Roberts and Anthony J. Mayo, "Toward a Racially Just Workplace," hbr.org, November 14, 2019, https://hbr.org/2019/11/toward-a-racially-just-workplace.

3. Center for WorkLife Law, "Pinning Down the Jellyfish: The Workplace Experiences of Women of Color in Tech," April 2022, https://worklifelaw.org/wp-content/uploads/2022/04/Pinning-Down-the-Jellyfish-The-Workplace-Experiences-of-Women-of-Color-in-Tech.pdf.

## Chapter 2

1. Jennifer L. Glass et al., "What's So Special about STEM? A Comparison of Women's Retention in STEM and Professional Occupations," *Social Forces* 92, no. 2 (December 2013): 723–756.

2. Women in the Workplace 2015 report, https://womenintheworkplace.com/2015.

3. Herminia Ibarra, "To Close the Gender Gap, Focus on Assignments," hbr.org, May 22, 2012, https://hbr.org/2012/05/to-close-the-gender-gap-focus-on-assignments.

4. Shelley J. Correll et al., "Inside the Black Box of Organizational Life: The Gendered Language of Performance Assessment," *American Sociological Review* 85, no. 6 (December 2020): 1022–1050.

## Chapter 4

1. Learnlight, "5 Reasons Why Diversity and Inclusion is Everybody's Business," Learnlight, February 27, 2018, https://insights.learnlight.com/en/articles/5-reasons-why-diversity-and-inclusion-is-everybodys-business/.

2. Claire Cain Miller, "Unintended Consequences of Sexual harassment Scandals," *New York Times*, October 9, 2017, https://www.nytimes.com/2017/10/09/upshot/as-sexual-harassment-scandals-spook-men-it-can-backfire-for-women.html.

## Chapter 6

1. McKinsey & Company, "Women in the Workplace 2021," https://www.mckinsey.com/featured-insights/diversity-and-inclusion/women-in-the-workplace; Tsedale M. Melaku and Angie Beeman, "Navigating White Academe during Crisis: The Impact of Covid-19 and Racial Violence on Women of Color Professionals," *Gender, Work & Organization*, March 5, 2022, https://onlinelibrary.wiley.com/doi/full/10.1111/gwao.12823.

2. Tsedale M. Melaku, "Why Women and People of Color in Law Still Hear 'You Don't Look Like a Lawyer,'" hbr.org, August 7, 2019, https://hbr.org/2019/08/why-women-and-people-of-color-in-law-still-hear-you-dont-look-like-a-lawyer.

3. Daphna Motro et al., "The 'Angry Black Woman' Stereotype at Work," hbr.org, January 31, 2022, https://hbr.org/2022/01/the-angry-black-woman-stereotype-at-work; Angie Beeman, "Teaching to Convince, Teaching to Empower: Reflections on Student Resistance and Self-Defeat at Predominantly White vs. Racially Diverse Campuses," *Understanding and Dismantling Privilege* 5, no. 1 (2015).

4. Tsedale M. Melaku, "The Awakening: The Impact of Covid-19, Racial Upheaval, and Political Polarization on Black Women Lawyers," *Fordham Law Review* 89 (2021).

5. Erving Goffman, *Stigma: Notes on the Management of Spoiled Identity* (New York: Simon & Schuster, 1963).

6. Lisa B. Spanierman and Laura Smith, "Roles and Responsibilities for White Allies: Implications for Research, Teaching, and Practice," *The Counseling Psychologist* 45, no. 5 (2017): 606–617.

7. Angie Beeman, "'If Only We Are Brave Enough to Be It': Demanding More from Diversity, Equality, and Inclusion Efforts to Support Women Faculty of Color," *Critical Sociology* 47, no. 7–8 (2021): 1099–1109.

8. Patricia Hill Collins, *Black Feminist Thought: Knowledge, Consciousness, and the Politics of Empowerment* (New York: Routledge, 2000).

9. Yanick St. Jean and Joe R. Feagin, *Double Burden: Black Women and Everyday Racism* (New York: Routledge, 2015).

## Chapter 7

1. Steven J. Spencer, Christine Logel, and Paul G. Davies, "Stereotype Threat," *Annual Review of Psychology* 67 (2016): 415–437.

2. Steven J. Spencer, Claude M. Steele, and Diane M. Quinn, "Stereotype Threat and Women's Math Performance," *Journal of Experimental Social Psychology* 35, no. 1 (1999): 4–28.

3. Wei Zheng, Ronit Kark, and Alyson L. Meister, "Paradox versus Dilemma Mindset: A Theory of How Women Leaders Navigate the Tensions between Agency and Communion," *Leadership Quarterly* 29, no. 5 (2018): 584–596.

4. Francesca Gino, *Rebel Talent: Why It Pays to Break the Rules at Work and in Life* (New York: Dey Street Books, 2018).

5. *Time*, "Firsts: Women Who Are Changing the World," https://time.com/collection/firsts/4899130/ava-duvernay-firsts/.

## Chapter 10

1. Sylvia Ann Hewlett, *Forget a Mentor, Find a Sponsor: The New Way to Fast-Track Your Career* (Boston: Harvard Business Review Press, 2013).

## Chapter 11

1. Jennica R. Webster et al., "'Dirty' Workplace Politics and Well-Being: The Role of Gender," *Psychology of Women Quarterly* 42, no. 3 (2018): 361–377; Mahmood Ahmad Bodla and Rizwan Qaiser Danish, "The Gender Differences in the Relationship between Perceptions of Organizational Politics and Work Performance," *International Journal of Knowledge Culture and Change Management Annual Review* 8, no. 6 (2008).

2. Takuma Kimura, "A Review of Political Skill," *International Journal of Management Reviews* 17, no. 3 (2015): 312–332.

3. Cynthia Hess, Tanima Ahmed, and Jeff Hayes, "Providing Unpaid Household and Care Work in the United States: Uncovering Inequality," Institute for Women's Policy Research briefing paper no. C487, January 2020, https://iwpr.org/wp-content/uploads/2020/01/IWPR-Providing-Unpaid-Household-and-Care-Work-in-the-United-States-Uncovering-Inequality.pdf.

4. Shawn Achor, "Do Women's Networking Events Move the Needle on Equality?," hbr.org, February 13, 2018, https://hbr.org/2018/02/do-womens-networking-events-move-the-needle-on-equality.

5. Alex M. Wood et al., "The Authentic Personality: A Theoretical and Empirical Conceptualization and the Development of the Authenticity Scale," *Journal of Counseling Psychology* 55, no. 3 (2008): 385–399.

6. Jessica Nordell, "This Is How Everyday Sexism Could Stop You from Getting That Promotion," *New York Times*, October 14, 2021, https://www.nytimes.com/interactive/2021/10/14/opinion/gender-bias.html.

7. Gregory M. Walton and Geoffrey L. Cohen, "A Question of Belonging: Race, Social Fit, and Achievement," *Journal of Personality and Social Psychology* 92, no. 1 (2007): 82–96.

## Chapter 14

1. Joseph Grenny, David Maxfield, and Andrew Shimberg, "How to Have Influence," *MIT Sloan Management Review*, October 1, 2008, https://sloanreview.mit.edu/article/how-to-have-influence/.

## Chapter 15

1. Kelly Greene (@kgreene90), "Sad to see not much has changed since I entered the field of male dominated engineering only to hear repeatedly 'you don't look like an engineer,'" Twitter, April 15, 2021, https://twitter.com/kgreene90/status/1382673533638172673.

2. Julie Hurst (@JulieWLBC), "Going back some time I was a journalist. The friend of one of my (male) colleagues came to meet him for lunch and got shown the news room. He was surprised when I was introduced as a reporter. Said he assumed the women were there to type up the stories for the men," Twitter, April 16, 2021, https://twitter.com/JulieWLBC/status/1383132512302600197.

3. Jenine McCutcheon (@jen_mccutcheon), "Having been injured at work by a (young white male) staff member who wasn't listening to me in my own lab. . . I won't be sharing that sentiment," Twitter, November 26, 2021, https://twitter.com/jen_mccutcheon/status/1464232302301650944.

4. Uché Blackstock (@uche_blackstock), "For the umpteenth time, I was asked again today by a parking garage attendant (**looking at my MD license plate for hospital parking), 'Are you the doctor or is your husband?'" Twitter, September 12, 2021, https://twitter.com/uche_blackstock/status/1437202726304288768.

5. Jennifer Huang (@drjhuang), "During my fellowship welcome picnic, I was mistaken as my co-fellow's girlfriend/wife and not one of the 2 starting fellows. Best of luck to all the women entering new training spaces this July! You belong. #WomenInMedicine," Twitter, June 29, 2021, https://twitter.com/drjhuang/status/1409928426681626624; Nancy Yen Shipley (@_NancyMD), "I was mistaken as a wife at a fellowship interview. I mean, I'm a wife. Of someone else. Who is not at the fellowship mixer. #weareallortho #orthotwitter," Twitter, June 30, 2021, https://twitter.com/_NancyMD/status/1410222523065634818.

6. Kalani Pickhart (@kalanipickhart), "I work as a staff person at a university and whenever a faculty person finds out I have a novel coming out, you can see their brain short-circuit like, 'wait, you're not supposed to be capable of anything but making my copies,'" Twitter, August 25, 2021, https://twitter.com/kalanipickhart/status/1430579748019703812.

7. Marcus Noland and Tyler Moran, "Study: Firms with More Women in the C-Suite Are More Profitable," hbr.org, February 8, 2016, https://hbr.org/2016/02/study-firms-with-more-women-in-the-c-suite-are-more-profitable.

8. Julie Hurst (@JulieWLBC), "On the plus side once had an employee who got sick of people assuming he was in charge and I worked for him. In public he frequently addressed me as 'boss' rather than my name. It got the point across and made us smile as we actually had a very informal relationship," Twitter, April 16, 2021, https://twitter.com/JulieWLBC/status/1383177880549609476.

9. Amani Jambhekar (@AjvictoryMD), "He was spooked by the look on my face and my tone of voice and he immediately changed course and said, 'Thank you ma'am for everything,'" Twitter, April 15, 2021, https://twitter.com/AjvictoryMD/status/1382671609996054530.

## Chapter 16

1. Leslie Ashburn-Nardo et al., "Do You Say Something When It's Your Boss? The Role of Perpetrator Power in Prejudice Confrontation," *Journal of Social Issues* 70, no. 4 (2014): 615–636.

2. Aneeta Rattan, "Confronting a Biased Comment Can Increase Your Sense of Belonging at Work," hbr.org, May 4, 2018, https://hbr.org/2018/05/confronting-a-biased-comment-can-increase-your-sense-of-belonging-at-work.

## Chapter 17

1. Amber L. Stephenson, Leanne M. Dzubinski, and Amy B, Diehl, "A Cross-Industry Comparison of How Women Leaders Experience Gender Bias," *Personnel Review*, https://doi.org/10.1108/PR-02-2021-0091.

2. M. Biernat and D. Kobrynowicz, "Gender- and Race-Based Standards of Competence: Lower Minimum Standards but Higher Ability Standards for Devalued Groups," *Journal of Personality and Social Psychology* 72, no. 3 (1997): 544–557.

3. Eden B. King, "The Effect of Bias on the Advancement of Working Mothers: Disentangling Legitimate Concerns from Inaccurate

Stereotypes as Predictors of Advancement in Academe," *Tavistock Institute* 61, no. 12 (2008): 1677–1711.

4. Sharon Mavin and Gina Grandy, "Women Elite Leaders Doing Respectable Business Femininity: How Privilege Is Conferred, Contested, and Defended through the Body," *Gender, Work & Organization* 23, no. 4 (2016): 379–396.

## Chapter 18

1. Jennifer K. Bosson and Joseph A. Vandello, "Hard Won and Easily Lost: A Review and Synthesis of Theory and Research on Precarious Manhood," *Psychology of Men & Masculinity* 14, no. 2 (2013): 101–113; Natalya Alonso, "Playing to Win: Male–Male Sex-Based Harassment and the Masculinity Contest," *Journal of Social Issues* 74, no. 3 (2018): 477–499.

2. Bosson and Vandello, "Hard Won and Easily Lost"; Louise Marie Roth, *Selling Women Short: Gender and Money on Wall Street* (Princeton, NJ: Princeton University Press, 2015); Katherine C. Kellogg, *Challenging Operations: Medical Reform and Resistance in Surgery* (Chicago: University of Chicago Press, 2011); Jennifer L. Berdahl, "Harassment Based on Sex: Protecting Social Status in the Context of Gender Hierarchy," *Academy of Management Review* 32, no. 2 (2007).

3. Joan C. Williams, Jennifer L. Berdahl, and Joseph A. Vandello, "Beyond Work-Life 'Integration,'" *Annual Review of Psychology* 67 (2016): 515–539.

4. Shannon L. Rawski and Angela L. Workman-Stark, "Masculinity Contest Cultures in Policing Organizations and Recommendations for Training Interventions," *Journal of Social Issues* 74, no. 3 (2018): 607–627.

5. Robin J. Ely and Debra E. Meyerson, "An Organizational Approach to Undoing Gender: The Unlikely Case of Offshore Oil Platforms," *Research in Organizational Behavior* 30 (2010): 3–34.

6. Amy Edmondson, "Psychological Safety and Learning Behavior in Work Teams," *Administrative Science Quarterly* 44, no. 2 (1999): 350–383.

7. Christin L. Munsch et al., "Everybody But Me: Pluralistic Ignorance and the Masculinity Contest," *Journal of Social Issues* 74, no. 3 (2018): 551–578.

## Chapter 19

1. Promundo-US, "So, You Want to be a Male Ally for Gender Equality? (And You Should): Results from a National Survey, and a Few Things You Should Know," Promundo, 2019.

2. NCWIT, "Male Advocates and Allies: Promoting Gender Diversity in Technology Workplaces," April 24, 2013, https://ncwit.org/resource/maleadvocateindustry/.

3. American Psychological Association, "APA Guidelines for Psychological Practice with Boys and Men," August 2018, https://www.apa.org/about/policy/boys-men-practice-guidelines.pdf.

4. A. K. Sesko and M. Biernat, "Prototypes of Race and Gender: The Invisibility of Black Women," *Journal of Experimental Social Psychology* 46, no. 2 (2010): 356–360.

5. Emma Hinchliffe, "Female Employees Who Are the Only Woman at Work Are 50% More Likely to Consider Quitting," *Fortune*, October 23, 2018, https://fortune.com/2018/10/23/women-only-one-lean-in-survey/.

6. Sahana Dharmapuri and Jolynn Shoemaker, "Feeling Guilty About #MeToo? Three Ways Men Can Do Something About It," *Ms.*, April 13, 2018, https://msmagazine.com/2018/04/13/feeling-guilty-metoo-three-ways-men-can-something/.

# INDEX

# Discussion Guide

Since the *Women at Work* podcast first launched, we've heard from all over the world that it has inspired discussions and listening groups. We hope that this book does the same—that you'll want to share what you've learned with others. The questions in this discussion guide will help you talk about the challenges women face in the workplace and how we can work together to overcome them.

You don't need to have read the book from start to finish to participate. To get the most out of your discussion, think about the size of your group. A big group has the advantage of spreading ideas more widely—whether throughout your organization or among your friends and peers—but might lose some of the honesty and connection a small group would have. You may want to assign someone to lead the discussion to ensure that all participants are included, especially if some attendees are joining virtually. And it's a good idea to establish ground rules around privacy and confidentiality. *Women at Work* topics touch on difficult issues surrounding sexism and racism, so consider using trigger warnings.

Finally, think about what you want to accomplish in your discussion. Do you want to create a network of mutual support? Hope to disrupt the status quo? Or are you simply looking for an empathetic ear? With your goals in mind, use the questions that follow to advance the conversation about women at work.

1. What are the dynamics like between men and women in your organization? Do you feel men and women are perceived as equals and given the same opportunities and assignments?

2. Does your organization see itself as gender equitable? Do women have a path to leadership positions? What systems or policies are in place to ensure equitable conditions and opportunities for women? Are they effective?

3. In chapter 1 Teresa Cardador describes a feeling of "outsider status" for women in male-dominated industries. Is this something you've experienced in your workplace? How has it changed the way you work with colleagues and team members? How has it affected your confidence and professional growth?

4. Describe a time when you observed or experienced healthy competition at work and a time when you observed or experienced unhealthy competition. What differentiated these two instances? What dynamics were at play that made one healthy and one not? Were they between men, women, or a mix?

5. What support exists for women in your organization? Are there mentors, sponsors, and allies available? What qualities do they have that you can recognize, and what actions are they taking—particularly men—to show that they're trying to make the workplace better? How would you recommend making a connection with them to partner together?

6. In chapter 5 we see a detailed account of the sponsorship relationship between Christina Massa and Julia González Romero. Are you a sponsor or a protégé? If so, what parts of Christina and Julia's relationship sounded similar to your partnerships? What aspects of their arrangement do you hope to build in your professional relationships? If you're not yet in a sponsorship relationship, what do you hope to find in a potential protégé or sponsor after seeing their example?

7. Describe a time where you've held back because you were experiencing imposter syndrome. How did you feel in the moment, and how do you feel about it now upon reflection? If you could go back, how would you have acted differently?

8. In chapter 9 Stacey Abrams and Lara Hodgson share how they leverage their differences—their gender, their race—in male-dominated spaces. Lara mentions making it her "superpower" by wearing a "statement necklace" and saying "something bold that makes the

audience uncomfortable." Where do you think this approach could work in your favor? Are there instances where you would worry this could backfire? Why?

9. Do you feel comfortable promoting yourself and your accomplishments at work? Where do you struggle? What parts of this process make you feel uncomfortable? What are ways that you can overcome this feeling so self-promotion feels more natural to you?

10. Share a time where someone has doubted your expertise, knowledge, or authority. Do you feel this was because of your gender, or something else? Did you respond, and if so, how? How would you navigate this type of situation in the future?

11. Describe a moment when someone said something biased or sexist in your workplace. Is this common in your organization? Did you or anyone else speak up at the time? How was it handled—or was it handled at all?

12. Has your boss ever said anything inappropriate or biased to you? How did you react? If you brought it up to your boss, how did the conversation go? Was your boss open to your feedback? What tips do you have for someone who faces this situation in the future?

13. Do you feel your organization has a masculinity contest culture? What behaviors lead you to feel this way? Are there certain phrases that colleagues commonly

use that feel especially masculine? How have you adapted your behavior to work in this type of culture? Where would you want to see the culture improve—or does it need to?

14. In chapter 19 W. Brad Johnson and David G. Smith describe situational awareness, with which men perceive the gender dynamics at play. Do you feel the men in your organization are situationally aware? What can you do to help them better understand what is going on? If you're a man, what steps can you take to increase your situational awareness?

15. Throughout the book, we heard that industries and organizations need to change in order to break the systemic biases in place. Who do you feel is responsible for making sure this happens, and how do you recommend they get started? What are some steps you can take to help?

## ABOUT THE CONTRIBUTORS

**Amy Bernstein, *Women at Work* cohost,** is the editor of *Harvard Business Review* and vice president and executive editorial director of Harvard Business Publishing. Follow her on Twitter @asbernstein2185.

**Emily Caulfield, *Women at Work* cohost (seasons 6–7),** is a freelance designer and runs a vintage clothing business, Still Cute Vintage. She was previously a senior designer at *Harvard Business Review.* Before pursuing a career in design, she held administrative roles in public education and the arts.

**Amy Gallo, *Women at Work* cohost,** is a contributing editor at *Harvard Business Review* and the author of *Getting Along: How to Work with Anyone (Even Difficult People)* and the *HBR Guide to Dealing with Conflict* (both Harvard Business Review Press, 2022 and 2017, respectively). She writes and speaks about workplace dynamics. Watch her TEDx talk on conflict and follow her on Twitter @amyegallo.

**Amanda Kersey, *Women at Work* producer,** is a senior audio producer at *Harvard Business Review.*

**Nicole Torres, *Women at Work* cohost (seasons 1–4),** is an editor at Bloomberg Opinion based in London and a former senior editor at *Harvard Business Review.*

**Stacey Abrams** is an entrepreneur, politician, and author. She is a coauthor of *Level Up: Rise Above the Hidden Forces Holding Your Business Back* and the cofounder of Now®.

**Carmen Acton** is a leadership impact coach and process consultant in the San Francisco Bay Area, California. Carmen has worked in a succession of corporate leadership roles in a variety of disciplines, ranging from safety engineering to employee and leadership development. She has worked with clients in sectors including oil and gas, food and beverage, technology, and health care.

**Jennifer L. Berdahl** is a professor of sociology at the University of British Columbia. Her research focuses on sexual harassment and organizational culture. She has worked with various organizations, in both the United States and Canada, to reduce harassment and discrimination.

**Vanessa Bohns** is a professor of organizational behavior at Cornell University and the author of *You Have*

*More Influence Than You Think.* Learn more about her research on social influence and persuasion at vanessabohns.com.

**Cynthia Burks** is a senior vice president and chief people and culture officer at Genentech.

**Teresa Cardador** is an associate professor of labor and employment relations at the University of Illinois Urbana-Champaign. Her research focuses on identity, meaningfulness, and gender at work; she is particularly interested in these issues as they relate to the work and career experiences of women in male-dominated occupations.

**Dorie Clark** is a marketing strategist and keynote speaker who teaches at Duke University's Fuqua School of Business. She has been named one of the top 50 business thinkers in the world by Thinkers50. Her latest book is *The Long Game: How to Be a Long-Term Thinker in a Short-Term World* (Harvard Business Review Press, 2021). Learn more and access free resources at dorieclark.com.

**Alisa Cohn** is an executive coach who specializes in working with *Fortune* 500 companies and prominent startups, including Google, Microsoft, DraftKings, Venmo, and Etsy. She is the author of *From Start-Up to Grown-Up.* Learn more at AlisaCohn.com.

**Marianne Cooper** is a senior research scholar at the VMware Women's Leadership Innovation Lab at Stanford University. Her book, *Cut Adrift: Families in Insecure Times*, examines how families are coping in an insecure age.

**Shelley J. Correll** is the Michelle Mercer and Bruce Golden Family Professor of Women's Leadership and the director of the VMware Women's Leadership Innovation Lab at Stanford University.

**Julie Diamond** is the CEO and founder of Diamond Leadership, which provides leadership and talent development services, including coaching, consulting, assessment, and training, to global clients. She is the author of *Power: A User's Guide.*

**Amy Diehl** is the chief information officer at Wilson College and a workplace gender bias expert and consultant. Find her on Twitter @amydiehl and visit her website at amy-diehl.com.

**Leanne M. Dzubinski** is the interim dean of the Cook School of Intercultural Studies, an associate professor of intercultural education and studies at Biola University, and a prominent researcher on women in leadership.

**Francesca Gino** is a behavioral scientist and the Tandon Family Professor of Business Administration at Harvard

Business School. She is the author of the books *Rebel Talent: Why It Pays to Break the Rules at Work and in Life* and *Sidetracked: Why Our Decisions Get Derailed, and How We Can Stick to the Plan*. Follow her on Twitter @francescagino.

**Peter Glick** is the Henry Merritt Wriston Professor in the Social Sciences at Lawrence University and a senior scientist with the NeuroLeadership Institute. He specializes in how organizations can overcome barriers to women's leadership and create a more optimal organizational culture.

**Julia González Romero** is an administrative and energy lawyer at Gonzalez Calvillo, an elite law firm in Mexico City. She is a board member at Voz Experta, an organization aiming to empower women in male-dominated economic sectors. She is a columnist for *Oil and Gas* magazine, *Energía Hoy*, and *Petróleo&Energía* and is a frequent public speaker.

**Joseph Grenny** is the coauthor of the *New York Times* bestselling book *Crucial Conversations*. He is also a cofounder of Crucial Learning, a learning and development company that offers courses in communication, performance, and leadership.

**Kathryn Heath** is a managing director at Bravanti and coauthor of *I Wish I'd Known This: 6 Career-Accelerating Secrets for Women Leaders*.

**Lara Hodgson** is cofounder, president, and CEO of Now®, as well as a coauthor of *Level Up: Rise Above the Hidden Forces Holding Your Business Back.*

**Raven Hoffman** is a senior estimator at Syverson Tile & Stone, Inc. in Sioux Falls, South Dakota, and is an active member of the National Association of Women in Construction.

**Judith Honesty** is an experienced organizational development consultant specializing in facilitating executive team interactions. During her long career in organizational development, she has developed and implemented culture and leadership assessments and designed and delivered interpersonal skills trainings in the Americas, Europe, and Asia.

**Tucci Ivowi** is the chief executive officer and a founding member of the Ghana Commodity Exchange. Prior to this, she worked with Nestlé in various roles including managing director, business executive officer, and marketing communications director across 22 countries. A thought leader, Chartered Marketer, and international business leader focused on strategy, innovation, and business turnaround, her professional experience spans the United Kingdom, emerging markets of Southeast Asia, and Sub-Saharan Africa. Connect with her at tucciivowi.com.

**W. Brad Johnson** is a professor of psychology in the Department of Leadership, Ethics, and Law at the United States Naval Academy and a faculty associate in the Graduate School of Education at Johns Hopkins University. He is a coauthor of *Good Guys: How Men Can Be Better Allies for Women in the Workplace*, *Athena Rising: How and Why Men Should Mentor Women*, *The Elements of Mentoring*, and other books on mentorship.

**Mikaela Kiner** is a CEO, author, and executive coach. In 2015 she founded Reverb, which helps companies create healthy, inclusive cultures. Prior to Reverb, Mikaela held HR leadership roles at companies including Microsoft, Starbucks, Amazon, PopCap Games, and Redfin. She's the author of *Female Firebrands: Stories and Techniques to Ignite Change, Take Control, and Succeed in the Workplace.*

**Michelle King** is the director of inclusion at Netflix and the author of *The Fix: How to Overcome the Invisible Barriers That Are Holding Women Back at Work.*

**Rebecca Knight** is a senior correspondent at *Insider* covering careers and the workplace. Previously she was a freelance journalist and a lecturer at Wesleyan University. Her work has been published in the *New York Times*, *USA Today*, and the *Financial Times.*

**Lori Nishiura Mackenzie** is a cofounder of the VMware Women's Leadership Innovation Lab at Stanford University and the lead strategist of diversity, equity, and inclusion at the Stanford Graduate School of Business.

**Cristina Massa** is a partner at Gonzalez Calvillo, where she leads the antitrust practice. She was the first female equity partner of the firm and the first woman to sit on the firm's executive committee. She's a member of the D&I Commission, and a mentor and sponsor of younger attorneys. She has been awarded by major legal publications both as an antitrust expert and as a D&I leader.

**David Maxfield** is a *New York Times* bestselling author, keynote speaker, and leading social scientist for business performance. Prior to his retirement, he led the research function at Crucial Learning, a learning and development company with courses in communication, performance, and leadership. His work has been translated into 28 languages, is available in 36 countries, and has generated results for 300 of the *Fortune* 500.

**Tsedale M. Melaku** is a sociologist, an assistant professor at the Zicklin School of Business at Baruch College (CUNY), and the author of *You Don't Look Like a Lawyer: Black Women and Systemic Gendered Racism*. Follow her on Twitter @TsedaleMelaku.

**Lesli Mones** is an executive coach, a leadership consultant, and the founder of the P2 Leaderlab, which helps women use their personal power skillfully for greater organizational impact.

**Aneeta Rattan** is an associate professor of organizational behavior at London Business School and cofounder of the Career Equally Newsletter. Her research focuses on mindsets and diversity, addressing stereotyping, prejudice, and inequity in the workplace with a focus on identifying how mindsets shape people's responses to experiences with overt and subtle biases.

**Leah Sheppard** is an associate professor of management in the Carson College of Business at Washington State University. She has taught courses in the areas of management, organizational behavior, leadership, and negotiations, and conducts research on the topic of gender stereotyping in the workplace. Her research has been featured in several outlets, including the *Atlantic*, the *New York Times*, *Forbes*, and the *Wall Street Journal*. In addition to research and teaching, she enjoys delivering corporate presentations about workplace bias and performance coaching services.

**David G. Smith** is an associate professor in the Johns Hopkins Carey Business School. He is a coauthor, with W. Brad Johnson, of *Good Guys: How Men Can Be*

*Better Allies for Women in the Workplace* and *Athena Rising: How and Why Men Should Mentor Women.*

**Amber L. Stephenson** is an associate professor of management in the David D. Reh School of Business at Clarkson University. Her research focuses on how professional identity influences attitudes and behaviors and how women leaders experience gender bias.

**Brenda F. Wensil** is managing director and head of the leadership acceleration practice for Bravanti. She is coauthor of *I Wish I'd Known This: 6 Career-Accelerating Secrets for Women Leaders.*

**Christoph Winkler** is the endowed professor and founding program director of the Hynes Institute for Entrepreneurship and Innovation at Iona College. Follow him on Twitter @VEntreship.

**Lisa Zigarmi** is an organizational psychologist and leadership coach. She helps leaders relate more deeply, decide more efficiently, and think with more creativity. She is the founder of The Consciousness Project.

# Women *at* Work

*Inspiring conversations, advancing together*

## ABOUT THE PODCAST

Women face gender discrimination throughout our careers. It doesn't have to derail our ambitions—but how do we prepare to deal with it? There's no workplace orientation session about narrowing the wage gap, standing up to interrupting male colleagues, or taking on many other issues we encounter at work. So HBR staffers Amy Bernstein and Amy Gallo are untangling some of the knottiest problems. They interview experts on gender, tell stories about their own experiences, and give lots of practical advice to help you succeed in spite of the obstacles.

**Listen and subscribe:**

Apple Podcasts, Google Podcasts, Spotify, RSS